D1331807

ADVANCED
OPERATIONS
MANAGEMENT

Second Edition

WITHDRAWN
FROM THE LIBRARY OF
UNIVERSITY OF ULSTER

100501054

The Securities & Investment Institute

Mission Statement:

> *To set standards of professional excellence and integrity for the investment and securities industry, providing qualifications and promoting the highest level of competence to our members, other individuals and firms.*

The Securities and Investment Institute is the UK's leading professional and membership body for practitioners in the securities and investment industry, with more than 16,000 members with an increasing number working outside the UK. It is also the major examining body for the industry, with a full range of qualifications aimed at people entering and working in it. More than 30,000 examinations are taken annually in more than 30 countries.

You can contact us through our website *www.sii.org.uk*

Our membership believes that keeping up to date is central to professional development. We are delighted to endorse the Wiley/SII publishing partnership and recommend this series of books to our members and all those who work in the industry.

Ruth Martin
Managing Director

ADVANCED OPERATIONS MANAGEMENT

Second Edition

David Loader

JOHN WILEY & SONS, LTD

100 501 054

658.5 VOA

Copyright © 2006   John Wiley & Sons Ltd, The Atrium, Southern Gate, Chichester,
West Sussex PO19 8SQ, England

Telephone (+44) 1243 779777

Email (for orders and customer service enquiries): cs-books@wiley.co.uk
Visit our Home Page on www.wiley.com

All Rights Reserved. No part of this publication may be reproduced, stored in a retrieval
system or transmitted in any form or by any means, electronic, mechanical, photocopying,
recording, scanning or otherwise, except under the terms of the Copyright, Designs and
Patents Act 1988 or under the terms of a licence issued by the Copyright Licensing Agency
Ltd, 90 Tottenham Court Road, London W1T 4LP, UK, without the permission in writing of
the Publisher. Requests to the Publisher should be addressed to the Permissions Department,
John Wiley & Sons Ltd, The Atrium, Southern Gate, Chichester, West Sussex PO19 8SQ,
England, or emailed to permreq@wiley.co.uk, or faxed to (+44) 1243 770620

Designations used by companies to distinguish their products are often claimed as trademarks.
All brand names and product names used in this book are trade names, trademarks or registered
trademarks of their respective owners. The Publisher is not associated with any product or
vendor mentioned in this book.

This publication is designed to provide accurate and authoritative information in regard to
the subject matter covered. It is sold on the understanding that the Publisher is not engaged
in rendering professional services. If professional advice or other expert assistance is
required, the services of a competent professional should be sought.

Other Wiley Editorial Offices

John Wiley & Sons, Inc., 111 River Street, Hoboken, NJ 07030, USA

Jossey-Bass, 989 Market Street, San Francisco, CA 94103-1741, USA

Wiley-VCH Verlag GmbH, Boschstr. 12, D-69469 Weinheim, Germany

John Wiley & Sons Australia Ltd, 42 McDougall Street, Milton, Queensland 4064, Australia

John Wiley & Sons (Asia) Pte Ltd, 2 Clementi Loop #02-01, Jin Xing Distripark, Singapore 129809

John Wiley & Sons Canada Ltd, 22 Worcester Road, Etobicoke, Ontario, Canada M9W 1L1

Wiley also publishes its books in a variety of electronic formats. Some content that appears
in print may not be available in electronic books.

British Library Cataloguing in Publication Data

A catalogue record for this book is available from the British Library

ISBN-13 978-0-470-02654-0 (PB)
ISBN-10 0-470-02654-5 (PB)

Project management by Originator, Gt Yarmouth, Norfolk (typeset in 12/16pt Trump Mediaeval).
Printed and bound in Great Britain by T.J. International Ltd, Padstow, Cornwall.
This book is printed on acid-free paper responsibly manufactured from sustainable forestry
in which at least two trees are planted for each one used for paper production.

To my wife and my colleagues who gave huge support to me in preparing this book and to all the operations managers past, current and future without whom there would be no financial services industry

CONTENTS

Appendices

PREFACE

· ·

Operations management is a vital component of any organisation in the financial markets. Without a highly efficient operational capacity any business would be vulnerable to competition and would find the overall cost of its business unviable. It is also the case that operations teams and the functions they perform have both altered radically in the last 5 to 10 years, illustrated by the active role in risk management that operations teams perform today. Traditionally a predominantly processing function, the changes to the structure of the industry have been significant and this has fundamentally altered the operations scope so that today its functions are both processing but also about risk control, client service, revenue or profit protection and in some cases revenue generation.

The fundamentals of operations management are still about accuracy, quality service and the ability to devise procedures to successfully clear and settle transactions. Today, the emphasis is also about effective asset and cash management, controlling risk and meeting the challenge of diverse and globalised trading and investment.

The high levels of sophistication of the so-called end-user in the fund management and retail markets creates the need for sophisticated services to be provided by banks and brokers as well as agents, custodians, depositories and clearing houses. The result of this has been significant rationalisation and revamping in most areas associated with the operations function.

Technology plays a major role in the operations function and yet it is the personal service that is still seen as of great importance, and this is increased where technology has had the effect of standardising processes and output. The ability to differentiate firms' products and services is a crucial business factor.

Advanced operations management is about the extra responsibility of business change management, identification of skill sets, development of multi-talented product and risk-aware teams of people, responding to fluctuating business demands, regulatory change and above all being aware of and responding to the ever intensifying competition.

It is not an easy role and it certainly demands multiple skill sets in the manager concerned but it can be an immensely satisfying role with real challenges and, increasingly, rewards.

The age of the professional in operations management is undoubtedly here and, importantly, it is widely recognised.

ABOUT THE AUTHOR

David Loader is actively involved in the international financial markets as a director of the Derivatives and Securities Consultancy Ltd, Computer Based Learning Ltd and Derivatives Management Services Ltd. He has over 30 years' experience in the financial services industry, much of the time at senior management level including operations director within major investment banks such as Warburg Securities, SBC Warburg and Warburg Futures & Options Ltd.

David is heavily involved with all three companies of which he is a director, providing a variety of services in training and consultancy to a broad base of clients world-wide. He designs and delivers training courses at all levels on many areas of the financial markets and, in particular, those related to operations. He has been commissioned to deliver programmes to audiences in a variety of countries for industry organisations – such as the Singapore Exchanges, the Stock Exchange of Thailand, the Australian Financial Markets Association and the Malaysian Exchanges. In addition to his work for clients in the UK, he has delivered training and consultancy in centres such as Milan, Prague, Singapore, Hong Kong, Boston, New York, Bermuda, Mumbai, Sydney, Johannesburg, Brussels and Frankfurt.

David is Managing Director of the Derivatives and Securities Consultancy Ltd, an affiliate member of the Securities and Investment Institute, a member of the Institute of Directors (*IOD*) and also a member of the Guild of International Bankers. Since 1999, David has been involved in CBL, which has been developed as a sister company to DMS Ltd. David is the senior author of CBL's *visUlearn* products, which cover the financial services industry. His practical knowledge of the financial industry is combined with his unique teaching ability, culminating in the innovative *visUlearn* range of multimedia training products.

Chapter

1

. . . .

THE CHALLENGE

In 1995 Nick Leeson changed the way operations would be viewed in financial institutions and markets forever.

In the late nineties Y2K highlighted the utter dependence of the markets on technology.

On 11th September 2001 the importance of disaster recovery and business continuation policies were graphically and tragically illustrated.

In 2002 the problems of Enron and the demise of its auditor, Andersen, in a little over seven months showed the consequences of reputation risk.

These were all headline making events and yet for the operations managers and directors involved, each one presented the kind of challenge, albeit on a more significant scale, which is faced daily in the process of settling business in the financial markets. Today outsourcing/insourcing, regulatory change, operational risk management and the wider use of more technical products in trading and investment are providing massive challenges for operations managers.

THE PROFILE OF OPERATIONS

Despite the phenomenal size of the market, settlement or the operations function is still often a little understood process. A bit like today's motor car which, to all intents and purposes, runs itself with virtually no involvement of the driver in maintenance, many in the trading environment and its support areas have little idea of what happens after the trade. Even fewer clients, particularly private ones, are aware of the vast mini-industry that enables those trades to be turned into realised profits or losses, dividends or unit trusts, insurance policies or mortgages. There are obvious reasons why the settlement process has become somewhat remote. Technology and automation have, in many cases, removed the need for paper evidence of ownership of securities or even cash. Collective investment schemes will buy and sell assets but this is irrelevant to the investor in terms of settlement because the manager deals with it, not them.

The way in which operations is used as an all encompassing term suggests that it is singular in format.

Similarly, the term 'bond market' suggests there is only one type of bond, which of course there is not.

People unfamiliar with the post-trade environment are often amazed at the complexity and diversification of the processes when they look into the subject. This is equally the case for people working in businesses that supply services to organisations in the financial markets such as technology companies that have large numbers of highly trained technical staff – e.g., programmers. In some companies their training will also include an understanding of, at least at a general level, what the client needs the technology for. These staff are often surprised at how critical and complex the various processes and procedures in the settlement chain are and correspondingly how important the systems are.

Operations in any type of organisation, be it a retail bank, broker, fund manager, custodian, fund administrator or an international investment bank, is a hugely complex function, dealing with many counterparts and systems and entailing many deadlines and actions that must be fulfilled.

OPERATIONS IS A BUSINESS

To be successful for a business, the operations function must be both efficient because it impacts on profit and loss (p&l) and controlled because it is a source of risk. A considerable part of its function is related to routine processes and procedures that apply to particular types of products or services. Record keeping, reconciling, payments and instructions are the everyday work of operations teams. For this reason some might suppose that it is predominantly an administration function, but that ignores the potential that operations has to be much more than just a supportive process. It has a product and any product has the potential to be sold and therefore to make money.

For instance, fund administrators and custodians make money out of operations-based services and they do so by developing and delivering efficient, cost-effective and above all innovative services to their clients in much the same way as a structured products team does in the front office environment.

Operations is in reality a business. It is as simple as that. It has an infrastructure, objectives, products and costs. Costs are high on the agenda in any business and that is very much the case in operations functions. Consider the following question. Why are there companies that insource the work of operations teams? The answer is because it is cheaper for the client to pay them than run a team themselves. The outsource/insource arguments are not solely based on cost issues but they are, nevertheless, a very significant consideration. Quality resource is another key business issue and, like effective cost management, the quality of resource is a vital component of a successful operations team. The outsource issue can be affected by the resource issue, particularly if the recruitment market is poor and quality staff are hard to get and very expensive. The inability to manage resource and cost will usually have only one outcome: once the cost of settling a bargain becomes too high, the operations team is vulnerable to comparison with an outsource option. This is a fairly clear challenge for the operations manager and their team.

Any type of business is unsustainable if it is making a loss. For years the cost of operations was accepted as a cost of doing the trading. It was absorbed as a service charge to the dealers. Naturally, managers were expected to manage the business as efficiently as possible, but whatever the cost, the front office underwrote it. Today, that is no longer the case. Operations is seen as an integral part of the business, a contributor to profits and losses, a cost that must be justified and stand up against comparison with competitors. It is no longer just accepted. Pressure is on the manager to deliver settlement performance, with the cost effectiveness that makes the service competitive in its own right and helps the competitiveness of the firm as a whole.

There are challenges because operations is a business, but there are also challenges from other sources including change.

THE CHALLENGE OF CHANGE

There can be no doubt that the global capital market infrastructure underwent an impressive amount of development and improvement over the last several years.

ISSA (2000) *Recommendations 2001 Status Report*

Change affects businesses, markets, regulation and individuals in different ways. A market change may boost trading and profit or commission but impact in a different way on operations by generating a possible problem. Change also creates both opportunities and resistance at staff level, and that can cause untold problems for the managers and supervisors. The performance of the procedures and processes, and the quality of the service delivered is still about people, however automated the business becomes. The people issue is the hardest to manage.

Most other problems can be relatively easily defined and solutions devised. That is not always the case with people. Even if the problem is easily defined, the solution may be difficult to find or implement. Any team needs stability and once a breakdown of the respect and coexistence of the staff, supervisors and managers happens, whatever the reasons for it, it is potentially disastrous. By way of example, even the introduction of extra headcount which, in normal circumstances, might reasonably be expected by the manager to prove a positive action, can in fact cause a far from positive reaction. A problem (shortage of resource) and its solution (hire extra staff) cause another problem (extra staff disrupt the accepted pattern). It appears to be a no win situation. Why is this the case? The manager needs to understand the workings of the operation and the minds of the staff and to recognise what motivates and de-motivates people. In the above example, extra headcount might not have been needed or possibly the salaries of the new staff were above those of existing staff, possibly the staff were simply not consulted and communicated with and so resentment was fostered. This may all seem fairly trivial but any manager that ignores the feelings and opinions of their staff is plunging headlong towards disaster.

So, we come to another challenge, management style.

THE CHALLENGE OF MANAGEMENT STYLE

Managers are people, not robots; so there is a different style for every manager depending upon their own particular personality. Football provides a good illustration of this. Some managers scream and shout even when their observations are totally wrong, mouth off in the media and are larger than life personalities. Others are more studious, think before they speak and loathe to be in the limelight. Two different ways of doing the job both of which can be successful or fail, depending on the type of people in the team and above all the skill of the manager to handle personalities, including their own.

It can also depend on the type of business, the workflow, the senior management style and the business strategy; in fact, so many influences can affect the manager and their style of management. Not surprisingly, their style can change as the manager experiences different situations and reacts accordingly. Some who start off being open and accommodating become tougher, whilst some who start with a firm 'I'm in total control' stance relax.

The secret is the ability to change in order to find the right level and then not to vary the style. Veering between 'tough' and 'approachable' unsettles staff completely.

Knowing when and how to delegate, empowering people, developing talent, motivating and being strong enough to deal with difficult situations that occur occasionally are all part of being a successful manager.

Challenges arise because operations is a business, and change happens.

Change is a key factor today in the industry and it is showing no sign of abating. The mergers of exchanges, clearing organisations, banks and fund management companies have a massive impact on the operations team. In the UK and elsewhere there have been changes to the regulatory environment. Europe has seen the introduction of the eurocurrency, the expansion of the EU and a significant fluctuation in the level of business as the major economies of the world experience variable growth.

THE CHALLENGE OF GLOBAL MARKETS

The impact of global markets cannot be underestimated. During 2002 the big pension and endowment policy providers had to deal with the result of exposure to falling equity markets and the impact that has had on their liquidity ratios and the performance of the investments.

Investors began to realise that better returns might be available in other forms of investment vehicles and the growth and development of hedge funds is a prime example of these alternative investments. The result has been a huge challenge to brokers, custodians and fund administrators to come up with services for these hedge funds. As they operate in a very different regulatory environment and can utilise many products that are more technical and 'exotic' than those used in traditional funds, the challenge to develop capabilities to manage valuations, accounting and reporting have been enormous.

With equity markets recovering we are also seeing significant increases in volumes across all markets and products.

In the hard world of finance, banks will only advance more funding to a life fund/pension firm if they see action being taken to reduce costs. The outcome is a reduction in headcount, even though it is proven that in the long run in many cases this course of action creates more problems. However, the operations manager doesn't run the firm and must deal with the consequences of the policies and strategies of the senior management. Managing this kind of scenario takes considerable skill. Maintaining morale, implementing the redundancy decisions and adjusting the procedures, processes and responsibilities, are all major challenges.

Enforced changes such as being required to reduce headcount can be difficult to manage for many reasons, but so too can managing a growth situation, or managing a major change to the processes. Gearing up for volumes that do not materialise can be just as bad as failing to position the team to deal with growth. The operations manager's judgement on how and when to move the function and the team forward is crucial.

What else is challenge?

THE CHALLENGE OF PERSONAL GOALS

Personal goals should include becoming a good manager, developing business skills and learning the technicalities of the job. Many managers possess either business skills or technical knowledge; it is surprising how few possess both.

It is important to recognise the need for both, in the supervisor as well as the manager. Fundamentally, it should extend to all staff and should be incorporated as part of the development of the team as a whole.

THE CHALLENGE OF DEALING WITH EVENTS

Operations as a function and the teams within operations are affected and influenced by events and circumstances generated from many sources (see Figure 1.1).

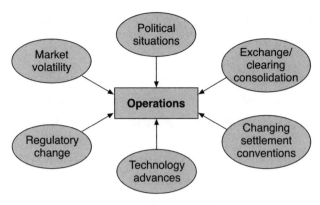

Figure 1.1   Industry influences.

Sometimes these events have as their source situations that will affect the industry universally and sometimes will impact on a specific part of the industry. Some events are of course from internal sources.

As can be seen from Figure 1.1 an event in this context is something that causes change or disruption. As the nature of the individual events can be very different in terms of profile and size or impact, the management of events is not straightforward. The worst case scenario is a major disaster or incident. For example, if SWIFT were to go down for a few days, chaos would ensue. Equally, settlement problems and internal technology problems can be significant. Risk is described in more detail in Chapter 3. In short, though, the manager must be able to:

- rapidly assess the impact of the event;
- communicate the details of the issue and the contingency;
- instigate the necessary changes to procedures;

- manage and monitor the function until the impact of the event is over.

Precisely what has to be done will, as noted, vary. There may be only a need for information and awareness of the event; on the other hand, action may be required.

This action could be anything from full-blown disaster recovery to temporary changes to procedures and processes. Managing change in technology, for instance, can be either complex or straightforward depending on the project. Similarly, managing resource and infrastructure may entail minor periodic changes; alternatively, it may entail full-scale headcount reduction or the management of a merger or takeover of or by another company.

Ultimately, all changes need organisational and leadership skill, depth of knowledge and flexibility. Achieving these is perhaps the first challenge the manager has; using them is the second.

One of a firm's greatest asset is its knowledge, its knowledge is its people, having someone successfully managing its people is perhaps the greatest asset of all.

David Loader

Chapter

2

....

THE MANAGEMENT PHILOSOPHY

Man is least himself when he talks his own person.
Give him a mask, and he will tell you the truth.

Oscar Wilde

Chapter 1 dealt with the challenges that operations managers face and the sources of the things and events that influence operations as a function and the operations team. But what is the management philosophy?

To understand the management philosophy certain key points should be considered:

- the type of operations function;
- the objectives for the management of the operation;
- the critical drivers for the business;
- how these will impact;
- other material influences.

Each of these points is instrumental in shaping the management philosophy. For instance, the operations manager in a small private client broker will have a smaller team and be much more involved in the workflow than the global operations manager in a major investment bank. Whilst there are fundamental processes and procedures that affect both the private client broker and the global investment bank, the methods of developing, implementing, running and controlling the two will be very different.

The manager in the private client broker will have far greater personal awareness of what is happening both in the business and in the operations function. The manager will be more hands-on in workflow and probably much closer to senior management, quite likely with a direct line to the senior directors or partners. As such, the manager will probably have significant scope for decision making and authority to act.

There will be a small team and the manager will know each person well. Communication will be fairly good and, despite the fact that the technology capability may be modest, there should be little likelihood of some problem growing unnoticed, at least for long. The small team will, from necessity, have multiple skills and day-to-day risk management should be reasonably straight-forward.

In contrast, the manager in the global investment bank is likely to have multiple reporting lines, large and possibly small teams in various locations, many personnel in the teams and a structure that will include junior managers and supervisors.

In addition, there will be business areas or departments so that skills may well be specialist and will be included within and across the teams. Communication will be more complex and the manager will rely heavily on information from his supporting junior managers and supervisors. The manager will have extensive technology at his disposal and will be receiving information about the overall business on a need-to-know basis from senior management. There will be scope for decision making related to general issues and day-to-day issues but more major decisions will probably need to be referred and/or incorporated into a matrix of decision making across the various business and operational areas within the organisation.

It should be relatively easy to see where and how the management philosophy will be different for these two organisations based on the assessment of positives and negatives. It should also be possible to see how the approach required to deal with them differs accordingly (Table 2.1).

Management structure plays a significant part in the process of operations management. Having a deputy and supervisors obviously reduces the individual's workload and in theory gives more control over the work and frees up the manager's time.

On the other hand, it is another thing that needs managing and sometimes it can create major problems for the

Table 2.1

Management issue	Small firm	Large firm
Personal contact with staff	**P** – small teams, easy to obtain input, convey and implement policy and deal with issues **N** – small source of input	**P** – wide source of input **N** – large teams and possibly several locations means reliance on deputies and supervisors to convey and implement policy
Multiple skill sets	**P** – teams tend to have broad range of under-standing and skill sets **N** – level of skill sets could be diluted	**P** – teams are often based on product lines, and a high level of awareness and skill sets exists for that product

Management issue	Small firm	Large firm
		N – teams tend to be specialist and have lower understanding of the broader picture associated with other products
Technology	P – few systems and relatively easy to train personnel in their use N – systems may lack wide functionality	P – systems may be sophisticated and highly functional N – could use different systems and there is heavy reliance on networking capabilities
Reporting lines	P – simple and easy to understand with clearly defined roles N – reliance on expertise of individuals	P – organisation gains wide input to management N – can be confusing and lead to assumptions that others are taking action; can also generate huge amounts of data for managers to deal with
Development and contingency	P – easy to train staff by sharing knowledge N – succession planning can be difficult and some skills may/will need buying in as training time may be limited	P – large teams allow for structured training and development and fast-tracking individuals N – personal progression expectations can be difficult to satisfy

Source: the**dsc**.portfolio.
N stands for 'negative', and P stands for 'positive'.

manager. Therefore, the management philosophy must be understood by all relevant parties and it must be consistent. Once responsibility has been devoted to a deputy, the manager should not continue to be involved. It confuses the situation and more importantly, it undermines the person to whom the work has been assigned. It is pointless for a manager to have a deputy if they are going to insist on becoming involved in everything that the deputy does.

It is understandable that a manager feels the need to protect or insulate themselves from the possible errors and repercussions that others may make, but this does not make it right.

Part of the management philosophy that is promoted in personal skills training concerns leadership. An operations manager is leading an operations team within an operations function. A manager who cannot develop people so that the function and the team can achieve their objectives is not a leader.

The management philosophy needs to be clearly stated by the firm, if it has multiple operations units and managers, as well as by the manager. The following elements will be included:

- structure of reporting lines;
- targets and objectives;
- responsibilities devolved;
- reporting requirements;
- budgeting;
- counterparties.

The manager needs to incorporate these into the team so that consistency and awareness are both evident in the actual day-to-day operational processes.

REPORTING LINES

This is a two-way issue: who the manager reports to and who reports to the manager. This is a simple concept, designed to allow the upward and downward movement of information, instruction and decision making, or in matrix management upwards, downwards and sideways. By having reporting lines, the onus for decisions is moved to the person deemed to be best to have that responsibility. In a simple scenario it looks like Figure 2.1.

Figure 2.2 shows a possible structure for the European, Middle East and Africa operations section of a global firm. Of course, all firms have their own specific structure, so this is purely illustrative but does show how quickly the responsibilities and reporting lines become expanded on

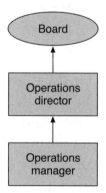

Figure 2.1 Reporting structure.

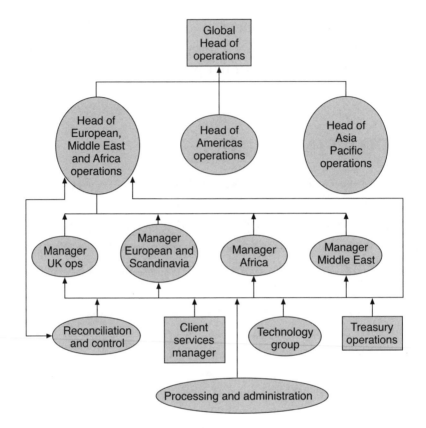

Figure 2.2   Enterprise-wide response structure.

and more complex. A similar structure would exist under the Americas and Asia Pacific regional centres.

It is vitally important for the manager to understand the importance of reporting line structures. Firms need to have control over situations and to be able to implement strategies smoothly and to respond to events. The reporting line procedure enables this to take place so that a responsibility is escalated to an appropriate level and each relevant person in the structure can oversee the day-to-day and more strategic situation giving adequate control. The process also allows ideas and observations to be channelled appropriately.

That is the theory behind the idea. However, if the structure becomes overly complex or does not function because it is ignored, problems will begin to manifest themselves.

The Bank of England's report into the collapse of Baring's commented on the structure and reporting lines within Baring's Bank. The sequence of events that led to the collapse of the Bank came about partly at least because of ineffective non-functioning reporting lines which resulted in the same person, Nick Leeson, being responsible for the operations function that supported his dealing.

The structure of an organisation and the approach to key strategies such as business development, client base and risk management will help to shape the management philosophy but it is still vitally important to recognise that the manager's own personality also determines the philosophy.

It will be seen in later chapters how this philosophy comes into play.

Chapter

3

....

THE MANAGEMENT OF RISK

The old believe everything, the middle-aged suspect everything, the young know everything.

Oscar Wilde

Seldom has so much time and money been devoted to understanding and managing risk as it is now in the financial markets industry. Of course, some kind of risk is actually part of a market such as insurance. Similarly, derivatives are used to hedge risk. This gives rise to issues like credit and market risk, both of which have been recognised since the 1960s.

Much more recent has been the identification of operational risk and within that operations risk. Driven by events like the collapse of Baring's and the causes of it, operational risk has risen in importance and the management of that risk is now the subject of regulatory requirements as well as the Basel Accord (see Appendix C).

What does this mean for the senior operations manager and the team?

First, it needs to be ascertained what operational risk is and how and where it impacts on the operations function.

Risk is an interesting subject. It is everywhere and manifests itself in many forms, some that are obvious, others that are less so. Risk can be an irritant or massively damaging. It is often ignored, sometimes feared and occasionally welcomed, the latter because it can offer an opportunity to profit from a situation. But risk is a diverse subject: the risk inherent in trading is different to the risk inherent in clearing and settlement.

Risk affects everyone in their personal lives; measures to reduce risk range from inoculation against diseases to life insurance. It is not easy to manage every risk to which people might be subject but prudent planning does reduce the likelihood of the risk and its attendant problems.

In essence, it is exactly the same in business. There are prudent measures that can be taken such as insurance and there are other actions that can be taken to protect a business from some of the risks it faces. The audit process will identify weaknesses, and disaster recovery programmes will enable business to continue in the aftermath of some catastrophic event. There are also the internal controls that will occur at various stages in the processes of the business, which are designed to prevent errors and ensure efficiency, and there are external controls which are aimed at reducing the risk of operating in markets, products and even countries.

The significant point, however, is that whilst extensive controls and protection can be introduced into our daily lives and businesses risk cannot be eradicated entirely. Errors occur, so accidents occur no matter how extensive or up-to-date controls are. Thus, rogue traders continue to surface even though many new regulations and controls were introduced after Leeson's devastating unauthorised trading destroyed Baring's Bank.

However, the objective of risk management is to:

1. Identify what the risks are.
2. Know the frequency of occurrence of the risk.
3. Understand how and where the risk will potentially impact.
4. Measure the impact of the risk.
5. Introduce the controls that will manage the risk

within the framework of the regulatory requirements and the risk appetite and policy of the business.

Risk is not a bad thing. Much of the trading activity that happens in the financial markets is about taking risk and profiting from risk strategies.

The difference is that the risk is recognised and, in theory, the exposure to that risk is monitored and managed. This risk is referred to as market risk.

MARKET RISK

The operations manager is involved in market risk, not specifically because of trading decisions and strategies but because of the bi-products of the dealing. This involves not only the clearing, settlement and accounting for the products but also the characteristics of the products. In fact, each of the following needs to be totally understood:

- the characteristics of the product(s) used;
- the market structure;
- the country(ies) risk profile for the products traded;
- the clearing and settlement structure;
- the regulatory and tax environments;
- the accounting issues.

These will be examined in greater detail.

CHARACTERISTICS OF THE PRODUCTS USED

Products tend to be classified as either vanilla or exotic, the former being fairly standard in composition and the latter more complex. There are many simple examples – e.g., a fixed income bullet bond, a convertible bond, a standardised exchange-traded call option and an over-the-counter average rate/Asian option.

Each product has a slightly different process associated with it because sometimes there is a predetermined outcome or a right to decide on an outcome and, on other occasions, there is a variable outcome and/or the need for a decision.

MANAGEMENT RISK

Managing risk is fundamental to the banking and securities business. Managers represent a risk in so much as their failure to perform damages the business and places it at risk. The following are both directly the responsibility of the manager.

INADEQUATE PROCEDURES AND CONTROLS

If a financial institution does not have written procedures and clearly defined organisational charts, it is easy for processes to be missed. These problems are aggravated if there are frequent organisational or process changes.

INFORMATION OR REPORTING RISK

Information or reporting risk is the risk that the reports and sources of information that management use to make their decisions contain incorrect or misleading information. Incorrect and misleading information can lead management to make wrong policy decisions and to make corrective action in the wrong direction. Misleading, distorted or delayed information can lead to trends or mistakes not being identified and, thus, ignored. Badly produced reports can lead to the incorrect amount of client money being segregated.

In both the above cases the manager directly influences the way in which the processes and procedures are devised and implemented for the functions.

There are of course other specific risks faced by financial institutions and these are examined next.

MARKET OR PRINCIPAL RISK

Market risk is the risk that changes in market conditions will have a negative impact on an institution's profitability. Examples of changing market conditions include changes to:

- interest rates, referred to as 'interest rate risk';
- foreign exchange rates, referred to as 'foreign exchange risk' or 'currency risk';
- the market value of investments held by the institution, which is sometimes referred to as 'price risk' or 'equity position risk' (in the case of equities).

Factors affecting market risk are the:

- length of time the position is held as there is a greater possibility of an adverse market price movement;
- liquidity or ease of resale when the level of risk becomes unacceptable for the holder. The longer it takes to find a buyer/seller the greater the risk of price movement;
- volatility of price fluctuations. Some emerging market equities have fluctuating prices whereas many gilts have relatively stable prices;
- sensitivity of the price to underlying factors. Derivatives prices move far quickly than the price of the underlying equity.

To evaluate its exposure to market risks, it is accepted that a financial institution should check the market value of its positions daily. Financial institutions should also compare this exposure with established market risk limits. Market risk is often measured and monitored by Value at Risk (VAR) models that use probability-based methodologies to measure the institution's potential loss under certain market conditions. VAR is a statistical measurement of the maximum likely loss on a portfolio due to adverse market price movements. It calculates the loss if the price moves by two standard deviations or 95%. It uses historical price movements to identify the probability of future adverse price movements. Another method is stress testing, which involves the application of extreme market movements that may arise as a result of hypothetical political or economic upheavals to a portfolio of investments.

'Mark to market' of all short positions at the bid price and all long positions at the offer price will enable a firm to ascertain its daily profit or loss. The mark to market value can be refined to take account of liquidity or settlement risk. Sensitivity analysis measures the degree to which the value of trading positions is vulnerable to changes in interest rates. Every future cash flow is discounted by the time value of money to give a net present value. The sensitivity calculation is usually expressed as the change in net present value of the portfolio produced by a 1 basis point movement in interest rates across the whole cash flow portfolio.

CREDIT OR COUNTERPARTY RISK

Credit risk is the risk that a customer will fail to complete a financial transaction according to the terms of the contract, resulting in a loss to the financial institution. In general terms, credit ratings are used in assessing the suitability of a counterparty and in most larger organisations a specialist credit department will deal with this.

Firms need to measure their credit risk and compare their exposure with predetermined counterparty limits. Credit risk measurements should reflect the impact of changing market conditions on the current and future ability of customers to meet contractual obligations. The evaluation of customer and counterparty creditworthiness, as well as the setting of individual credit limits, should be the responsibility of an independent credit department.

However, there is another type of counterparty risk.

It is also the possibility or probability that the operational performance of the client or counterparty will be substandard and will therefore impact negatively on the firm's own performance. Typically, this will include repeated late settlement or payments, and/or erroneous instructions. This can also be included under settlement risk (see following).

OPERATIONAL RISK

Operational risk is defined by the Basel Committee as 'the risk associated with human error, systems failures and inadequate procedures and controls during the processing of business related transactions.' Operational risk can be broken down into further sub-sections like reporting risk, malicious risk, legal risk and regulatory risk.

There are many types of operational risks including, but not restricted to:

- settlement risk;
- personnel/human resource (HR) risk;
- liquidity;

- financial risk;
- technology/system risk;
- legal risk;
- regulatory risk;
- reputation risk.

Settlement risk is a subsection of operational risk and relates to risks occurring within the settlement cycle. It is the risk that the transaction will not settle properly, that there will be a delivery of 'bad' stock, a late settlement or that one counterparty will default on their obligation (this is also a credit risk). Settlement risk is greatest in free-of-payment deliveries and foreign exchange (*FX*) transactions. With foreign exchange transactions, there is a risk of non-receipt of the purchased currency after irrevocable instructions have been passed to deliver the sold currency. Banks operating in different time zones and over public holidays and weekends further exacerbate this problem. Developments like CLS Bank (see Chapter 11) are designed to overcome the problems in FX markets.

Settlement risk is increased or decreased depending on the format of the clearing process. The central clearing counterparty (*CCP*) concept, where the clearing house becomes the counterparty to the trade, significantly reduces the counterparty risk whilst the traditional securities clearing process, where counterparties remain linked until settlement, causes potential problems, notably the risk of settlement failure. Also, there can be the 'chain effect' as there are frequently many interdependent transactions. For example, in Figure 3.1

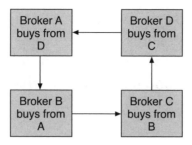

Figure 3.1   Settlement circle.

several transactions in TopStock plc have become inter-dependent on each other but in the process have become 'locked'.

Some clearing houses have procedures to overcome this locking or settlement circle situation. For instance, CREST runs a circles algorithm to resolve inter-dependencies.

MEANS OF REDUCING SETTLEMENT RISK

There are several basic ways in which settlement risk can be mitigated.

As with all risk there is a need for extensive knowledge of:

- products;
- market and clearing structure;
- settlement processes;
- payment processes;
- custodial processes;
- system capabilities.

There must also be an awareness of the effectiveness of the internal procedures and processes, how effective the controls are and what potential developments will impact positively and negatively on the risk position in the operations function.

One effective control over settlement risk is to ensure that delivery versus payment (*DVP*) settlement should be used as often as possible and in the case of collateral delivery versus delivery (*DVD*). Although free-of-payment settlement is inevitable in some circumstances, the controls over this should be such that it is authorised and monitored at all times.

As mentioned earlier, counterparty and settlement risk is further mitigated by the introduction of the CCP for securities settlement.

The London Clearing House (*LCH*) and Clearnet both provide a CCP, LCH for certain transactions on the London Stock Exchange (*LSE*) through CREST and Clearnet for Euronext.

It is important to understand the concept of CCP and how its introduction and role will impact on the operational workflow. Details of relevant papers pertaining to this can be found at The Futures and Options Association website: *www.foa.co.uk*

PERSONNEL/HR RISK

People are one of a firm's biggest assets; they are also a very substantial source of risk.

Why is this so?

Essentially, the involvement of people at various stages in the operations cycle leads to inevitable situations where the individual, or indeed team performance, may be less than adequate to alleviate risk. An example is the level of resource available to meet a volume of business. Another is the product awareness of individuals involved in key stages of the process. Personnel problems can be very difficult to manage and there is always the risk of simple, but potentially highly dangerous, human error. Examples of human error include inputting trade details incorrectly – e.g., a buy rather than a sell, 10 rather than 100, entering trades twice, running reports at the wrong time, forgetting to start information technology (IT) processes and failing to back up data.

A common phrase that is used in operations, and one that is frequently true is:

What can go wrong, will go wrong.

Human error is exacerbated by over-stretched staff in periods of high volume, staff absence due to illness and holidays, inexperienced staff and lack of clear written procedures. The latter is dealt with further in Chapter 8 and managing people in Chapter 6.

LIQUIDITY RISK

Liquidity risk encompasses two risks, one that might be defined as a market risk, the other as operational. First, it is the risk of not being able to sell or buy a security at a given time or at an acceptable price. This may be because of a lack of market participants (a thin market) or due to technical or operational disruptions in the market place. A prime example is a stock market crash with investors and institutions curtailing activity until volatility in the price of securities has reduced or a sustained bull run when there are many more buyers than sellers of stock. Second, there is also funding liquidity risk that relates to a firm's cash flow or asset position. If cash flow is insufficient to meet its payment obligations on settlement dates or margin calls, a firm will have very major problems. There are many implications.

In a CCP environment the failure to settle may constitute a default with the clearing house. Alternatively, the firm will be hit by claims or fines or both for failing to settle. In risk terms one party's funding or asset liquidity risk is another party's counterparty risk.

Ultimately, Baring's collapsed because they could not meet the margin calls on the Singapore Exchange for the derivatives positions that had grown to massive amounts as the Kobi earthquake made the futures price move unfavourably. Management in Baring's, not knowing the true extent of the positions and not verifying why so much capital was required, compounded the whole situation.

The collapse of Baring's was managed by the clearing house and the markets, but the impact could have been far more extensive than it was, although many firms experienced huge liquidity problems in funding and trading as banks reduced lending facilities and credit departments reviewed their exposure to counterparties immediately after Baring's demise. What everyone was concerned about was the possibility of other firms collapsing, referred to as 'systemic risk'.

SYSTEMIC RISK

As with most types of risk, systemic risk has a variety of formats. It is the ultimate liquidity risk whereby the default by one firm will cause further firms to default, leading to further firms defaulting until the whole system collapses like a set of dominoes – e.g., the Wall Street Crash of 1929. It is fear of the domino effect that causes the regulators, central banks and politicians to decide whether to step in to save firms or let them collapse. In the case of Baring's and Long Term Capital Management (*LTCM*) the decisions were different because the impact of the collapse of LTCM was much more likely to precipitate a global collapse in the financial markets.

However, systemic risk also occurs within a firm and within an operations function. The principle is the same. A problem starts in one part of the firm or operations area and quickly impacts on other parts. An example is problems with trade input or prices affecting the data sent to clients.

Risk rarely remains confined to one specific area or category and is therefore fluid.

A risk may arise in one area but its severe impact may be felt in another. Thus, the ability of the operations manager to identify source, cause and impact of operational risk is vitally important in the overall risk management process. An uncontrolled linked risk can ultimately create a disaster by becoming systemic and impacting elsewhere in an organisation.

Baring's is an example of this because the failure to deal with operational risk issues like segregation of duties, reconciliations and payment validation ultimately led to it going bust.

In global operations there is a likelihood that standards and practices may vary across different parts of an organisation. Controls and procedures must be robust enough to recognise this.

Being able to understand the impact of a risk within a firm and within the operations area is a crucial role for the operations manager. Devising methods to measure the impact of risk, like risk envelopes or portfolios, is vital.

FINANCIAL OR TREASURY RISK

In operations terms this is the inefficient use of cash and securities. Securities financing is covered in Chapter 4, but financial risk is also about penalties like fines and claims, etc., overdraft costs and lack of control over expenditure (particularly, expenses and consumables). There could also be loss if an injured party fails to claim benefits to which it is entitled.

Operations is a business and will have a budget. The manager must be able to prepare and control that budget effectively.

TECHNOLOGY RISK

Technology is both power and danger. It gives advantages that can be exploited and problems that can be devastating. It drives operations but can equally be a constraint and it can be costly if not managed correctly.

Of all the things that affect operations performance, technology is the biggest friend and, at the same time, a potential nightmare. Only managers that embrace technology and have the vision to develop it will be prepared for the changes and challenges that operations face in the coming years. Technology drives businesses, operations managers drive technology. Making it happen is the challenge for managers in both operations and technology. Technology risk is, not surprisingly, varied.

SYSTEMS FAILURES

IT and system problems can range from problems with programs – e.g., system affected by viruses, bugs or incorrect codes – to complete system failures when no trades can be input or processes can be run. IT problems are aggravated by new systems that experience teething problems and old systems that have problems coping with the volumes and complexity of the business. IT problems are worsened if a financial institution has many different systems and applications bolting on to one another.

TECHNOLOGY AWARENESS

One critically important goal for operations and technology managers has to be making the staff in their respective areas understand the roles, capabilities, issues and opportunities each area offers. Only if there is a good understanding of how operations function and how IT projects are managed and delivered will a really beneficial working relationship be established.

The relationship between operations and technology is considered in Chapter 7.

LEGAL RISK

Legal risk is the risk that contracts are not legally enforceable (*ultra vires*) or documented incorrectly, leading to a loss for the firm. An example of this is Hammersmith Council and the interest rate swap saga, where the council did not have the legal and necessary regulatory authority to engage in these transactions and, thus, the banks that were counterparty to the transactions had to suffer the loss.

Legal risk is linked to operations because of the many agreements that will exist between the firm and its counterparties. These agreements must be capable of protecting the firm in the case of disputes and problems at some stage in the relationship.

Typical agreements will be:

- service level agreements;
- stock lending agreements;
- prime brokerage/clearing agreements;
- custody agreements;
- client agreements;
- derivatives agreements
  - either clearing – i.e., agreements pertaining to the market – or
  - client – i.e., agreements between the broker and/or counterparty, such as ISDA documentation (see ISDA website: *www.isda.org*).

Operations will liaise with the legal department in all these cases, but managers must be aware of the contents of the agreements and how these impact on the function and the services provided and/or used.

REGULATORY RISK

Regulatory risk is the risk that a firm breaches the regulator's rules or codes of conduct.

In the UK the Conduct of Business (*COB*) rules set out, amongst other things, how to classify customers and, thus, what investments are suitable. The COB rules provide the content of the customer agreement letter, contract notes and advertising.

The client money and safe custody rules state how client money must be segregated and separately identified at all times. Segregated money is held in trust and, due to the trust rules, the exact client money must be segregated.

The financial resources rules set out how much capital buffer an institution must have to protect it from unforeseeable losses. The money laundering regulations state what steps a financial institution must undertake to prevent and identify money laundering; there are severe penalties for not complying with the procedures.

REPUTATION RISK

Reputation risk is more important than people frequently realise and can easily lead to the rapid decline of a company. Examples of this are Andersen in the aftermath of Enron, and Ratners following the Chairman's speech rubbishing the company's products. It is particularly important to companies with strong brand names and highly competitive markets and to new firms such as the Internet stockbroking companies.

A single error, ill-judged comment, missed performance standards, sloppy service delivery or a period of repetitive problems can undo years of building a reputation. Operations is at the front of the risk simply because it not only interfaces with external parties but also because it gen-

erates much of the critical administrative work associated with the firm, such as payments and information
distribution by which performance is judged.

Instilling the danger of reputation risk into the minds of
the operations team is crucial and the message needs
constant reinforcing. Setting internal standards for the
team and monitoring and then providing analysis to them
can achieve this. In this way the team are not only aware
of their performance but can also provide input to
maintaining and increasing standards.

OTHER RISKS

There are several other types of risk that the operations
manager must be aware of.

Malicious risk

All companies face the risk of fraud, theft and malicious
action against the firm's systems by employees, dis-
gruntled ex-employees, competitors and outsiders. There
are also an increasing number of computer hackers who
may seek to ruin a company. This is further evidenced by
demonstrations such as those by environmentalists and
the Stop The City demonstrations that hit cities such as
London and Seattle.

Country risk

International investment and trading portfolios contain
numerous products that provide good opportunities for

profit that may be issued and traded in emerging markets or markets where volatility is high. Emerging market or country risk is an important issue as there are likely to be heightened risk implications, particularly for operations.

These risks will typically be:

- market open to manipulation;
- rapid expansion of newly listed securities caused by the dash for growth;
- volatile trading activity;
- conflicting and ineffective (by mature market standards) regulatory environment and structures;
- lack of and poor quality information;
- physical share certificates;
- lack of automated settlement processes;
- fraud;
- low liquidity;
- limited number of counterparties offering custody and other services.

Given that the emerging markets do present trading and investment opportunities, it is inevitable that operations teams must overcome the settlement problems associated with such business. To achieve this, operations managers must familiarise themselves with the potential risks associated with each country and implement the necessary processes and controls to manage such business efficiently and safely. An example of the kind of problem that might arise is the action taken by Malaysia to protect its currency from speculators. By freezing any movement of capital from the country, profits on speculative investment and trading were effectively frozen and were also at risk from any fluctuation in the value of the Ringett.

Understanding risk

The best way to understand risks is to look at articles and reports on the major problems and events that have occurred in the industry and relate these to the business that you are involved in. Consider why things went wrong and how it could have been prevented and to what extent these were market, credit or operational risk (or any combination). Do your existing controls look strong enough to deal with such situations, particularly given the numerous changes taking place in the markets? Also, it is important to look at past internal problems and how these have been resolved.

Some of the major risk-related industry events include Baring's, the copper scandal at Sumitomo, star traders at Kidder Peabody, Morgan Grenfell, the Hammersmith and Fulham Local Authority interest rate swaps debacle and the problems over the default of Griffin.

It is worth looking at the Financial Services Authority (*FSA*) website and looking at the disciplinary actions taken against firms and individuals that have created unacceptable risk scenarios.

Controlling risk

It is essential that a financial institution has adequate controls in place to monitor and manage risk. A good internal control environment will cover the following areas.

Strategic controls

Organisational structure is a major control. All firms must have a clear organisational and reporting structure so that all employees know who to report to. All employees should know what tasks they are responsible for. When jobs are divided, there must be a clear allocation of duties.

While managing risks is important throughout an institution, specific responsibility for risk management falls to:

- the board of directors;
- the executive committee;
- the risk management group (risk manager in smaller firms);
- internal audit;
- compliance;
- operations managers.

The responsibility for understanding an institution's risks (and ensuring they are appropriately managed) is placed clearly with the board of directors. The board of directors must approve risk management strategies, but will delegate authority for day-to-day decisions to an executive committee so that risk can be effectively managed in the institution.

The board, through the executive committee, should identify and assess the institution's risks and develop a firm-wide risk management strategy to cover these risks. It should put structures in place to manage the quantifiable risks and to control the non-quantifiable risks.

Responsibility for capital allocation to business units/divisions also lies with the board. In the process, they should make use of an independent risk management group (RMG) to ensure that risks undertaken are within the institution's risk tolerance. The executive committee should maintain continuous and demonstrable compliance with applicable capital requirements.

The executive committee should evaluate the independence and overall effectiveness of the institution's control and risk management infrastructure on a regular basis. The executive committee should also initiate and maintain a set of risk limits to manage and restrict the maximum amount of risk across business units. This set of limits (e.g., capital at risk or VAR limits) should be approved by the board. In addition, the institution's organisational structure should have clear reporting lines and responsibilities to enable the executive committee to monitor and control activities.

The RMG should be independent with clearly defined responsibilities, reporting directly to the board or a special sub-committee. The internal audit function should evaluate and report on accounting and other controls over operations. Internal audit should be specifically charged with assessing, for each area it examines, the adequacy of the IT and other systems in operation, in relation to the risk management strategy adopted.

The board should also ensure that an adequate compliance department has been established, charged with managing the institution's compliance with financial and business conduct regulations on a global basis. In addition, the board should ensure that the activities of the institution are subject to frequent review by regulatory experts, so the business should not be exposed to material risk of loss due to breaches of regulations or failure to anticipate regulatory changes and issues.

The firm should ensure that all management, trading, operations, risk management and auditing activities are undertaken by professionals in sufficient number and with appropriate experience, skill levels and degree of specialisation.

MANAGEMENT RESPONSIBILITY

The FSA and other regulators are moving towards a culture of giving senior management more responsibility. Many regulated firms are using, or moving to, forms of risk-based compliance in order to focus scarce resources most effectively on the key business issues. Firms are therefore obliged to allocate responsibilities among the directors and senior managers and to ensure that the operations of the firm can be adequately monitored and controlled both by the senior managers and its governing body. Firms must take reasonable care to ensure that appropriate systems and controls are established and maintained.

ROLE OF RISK MANAGEMENT

The creation of operational risk management programs has been driven by management commitment, the need for an understanding of enterprise-wide risks, a perceived increase in exposure to operational risk and risk events, and regulatory requirements. In addition, there is an increasing need to demonstrate control over risk to potential clients and counterparties, so in some respects risk has become a commercial consideration. That can be used to a firm's advantage if they are fully committed to developing and managing operational risk.

In order to manage risk every firm must consider the following areas.

Strategy

Risk management begins with the determination of the overall strategies and objectives of the institution and the subsequent goals for individual business units, products or managers. Once strategies and objectives are determined, the institution can identify the associated inherent risks in its strategy and objectives. Both negative events (such as a major loss that would have a significant impact on earnings) and positives (such as profitable new products that depend on taking operational risk) are considered. A firm is then able to set a risk appetite. Specifically, it can determine what risks the company understands, will take and will manage versus those that should be transferred to others or eliminated.

Risk policies

Operational risk management policies are a formal communication to the entire organisation about the company's approach to operational risk management. Policies typically include a definition of operational risk, the organisational approach and related roles and responsibilities, key principles for management, and a high-level discussion of information and related technology.

The risk management process

This defines the overall procedures for operational risk management, which includes:

- definition of internal controls, or selection of alternate mitigation strategy, such as insurance, for identified risks;
- programs to ensure that controls and policies are being followed and to determine the level of severity. These may include process flows, self-assessment programs, and audit programs;
- a combination of financial and non-financial measures, risk indicators, escalation triggers and economic capital to determine current risk levels and progress toward goals;
- information for management to increase awareness and prioritise resources.

Risk mitigation

These are specific controls or programs designed to reduce the exposure, frequency or severity of an event. The
controls can also eliminate or transfer an element of
operational risk. Examples include business continuity
planning, IT security, compliance reviews, project management, and merger integration and insurance.

Operations management

The day-to-day processes of operations management,
such as front- and back-office functions, technology,
performance improvement, management reporting and
people management all have a component of operational
risk management embedded in them.

Culture

There is always a balance between formal policies and
culture, or the values of the people in the organisation.
In operational risk, cultural aspects such as communication, the 'tone at the top', clear ownership of each objective, training, performance measurement and knowledge
sharing all help set the expectations for sound decision
making.

In addition, the integration with market and credit risk in
an enterprise-wide risk management framework is noted,
as well as alignment with the needs of the stakeholders –
e.g., customers, employees, suppliers, regulators and
shareholders.

University
of Ulster
LIBRARY

Risk management departments

Some of the larger firms have evolved their operational risk management practices in a variety of ways depending on the culture and the organisation's operational risk event history.

One way of looking at the control of risk is to undertake a phased introduction of management.

First phase: The historical risk situation

Operational risks have always existed and are managed by focusing primarily on internal controls. They are the responsibility of individual managers in the business and specialist functions, with periodic objective review by internal audit. Traditionally, there is not a formal operational risk management framework.

Second phase: Developing risk awareness

Senior management must take an active role in increasing the understanding of operational risk in the organisation, and they must appoint someone to be responsible for it. To gain awareness, a common understanding and assessment of operational risks must exist. This assessment begins with the formulation of an operational risk policy, a definition and development of common tools. The tools in this stage usually include self-assessment and a risk process map. In addition, early indicators of operational risk levels and collection of loss events should be developed. These provide a common framework for risk identification, definition of controls, and prioritisation of issues and mitigation programs. However, the most important factor in this phase is gaining senior management commitment and the buy-in of ownership of operational risk at the business unit level.

Third phase: Measuring and monitoring risk

After identifying all of the operational risks, it is important to understand their implications to the business. The focus then becomes tracking the current level of operational risk and the effectiveness of the management functions. Risk indicators (both quantitative and qualitative) and escalation criteria, which are goals or limits, are established to monitor performance. Measures are consolidated into an operational risk scorecard along with other relevant issues for senior management. About this time, the businesses realise that the operational risk management process is valuable and assign dedicated staff to analyse processes and monitor activity. An operational risk program may be introduced.

With a better understanding of the current situation, it is time to focus on quantifying the relative risks and predict what will happen. More analytic tools, based on actual data, are required to determine the financial impact of operational risk on the organisation and provide data to conduct empirical analysis on causes and mitigating factors. Operational risk management is developing a comprehensive set of tools for the identification and assessment of operational risk:

- self- or risk assessment;
- risk mapping;

- risk indicators;
- escalation triggers;
- loss event database.

Fourth phase: Implementing controls

Recognising the value of the risk assessment undertaken by each business unit and the complementary nature of the individual tools, management focuses on integrating and implementing risk management processes and solutions. It balances business and corporate values, qualitative versus quantitative assessment and different levels of management needs. Risk quantification is by now fully integrated into the economic capital processes and linked to compensation. Quantification is also applied to make better cost/benefit decisions on investments and insurance programs. However, this integration goes beyond the processes and tools. In leading companies, operational risk management is being linked to the strategic planning process and quality initiatives. When this linkage is established, the relationship between operational risk management and shareholder value is more directly understood.

In many organisations a head of operational risk, reporting to the chief risk officer, is appointed. The role is to develop and implement the operational risk framework and consult with the lines of business. As has already been seen, the business units are primarily responsible for managing operational risk on a day-to-day basis. There are other risk-related functions (e.g., information technology, legal, compliance, HR) that have responsibility for specific operational risk issues. While the trend for market risk and credit risk is towards increasing centralisation, operational risk, by its nature, is more decentralised.

The operations manager needs to reflect that, whilst this is the case, there will still be a risk position to report and there may be requests for remedial action for approval. There can, depending on the organisation and its sophistication in risk management, be limits on activity and exposures to measure risk against.

Individual business units like operations have operational risk whether they like it or not, and cannot transfer the responsibility for management of it. The culture of the organisation, rather than the type of institution, determines the risk management approach and, as has been seen, there are three types of operational risk management structures that have appeared: a head office operational risk function, dedicated but decentralised support through areas and, finally, internal audit.

Staff training

One of senior management's greatest sources of risk management control is being able to rely on their staff and their knowledge because they are well trained, not just in terms of the firm's procedures but also in their general understanding of market practice. This addresses risk issues and has a spin-off since the provision of high-quality training to staff encourages their loyalty to the firm at the same time as giving them skills which are ultimately transferable.

While in the past the training spotlight has focused on the front office, many firms have realised that the formal training of back-office staff brings just as much to the firm in terms of efficiency of processing and the integrity of management controls.

Revenue is taken in the front office, but profits are made or lost in operations. Risk is part of business but operations can dramatically reduce the level of operational risk that undermines profits and increases losses and, ultimately, can result in the demise of the firm.

Chapter

4

....

SECURITIES FINANCING

Securities and cash are a fundamental part of the clearing and settlement process, custody, fund administration and prime brokerage. This is because every transaction in the market place involves the exchange of cash or securities in some combination in settlement of the deal. Cash is usable in the firm for trading or investment and its availability is determined by the efficiency of the operations function. The funding or cash inflow in respect of settlement, corporate actions and financing, like securities lending and borrowing, contributes to the money managed by treasury operations. In turn, the cash ladders for fund managers and traders alike is adjusted and then utilised. Any incorrect or unnecessary funding will therefore affect the efficiency and performance of the firm.

WHAT IS SECURITIES FINANCING?

Securities financing is about the use of securities and cash to maximise returns or reduce the cost of finance for trades and positions. Most assets have a value which means that they can be used for:

- lending;
- collateral;
- repurchase agreements;
- securitisation.

It may be safely assumed that the financial services industry can only operate at all because there are ways in which liquidity and the control of risk is made relatively easy for participants. If the need for ways to enhance the return on investments is added, it can be seen why the secondary use of securities is today a big part of the financial markets.

The secondary use of securities has been actively promoted by organisations like the International Securities Services Association (*ISSA*) as a means not only of adding liquidity to the markets but also of reducing the risk associated with settlement failures.

In purely commercial terms, the secondary use of securities is a lucrative source of business for organisations' custodians that hold copious amounts of securities on behalf of their clients and prime brokers who are servicing hedge funds. The custodians and, for that matter, the securities depositories can both help their clients to achieve returns whilst at the same time generating useful fees for themselves. The prime brokers need to be able to utilise securities both for covering short positions taken by hedge funds and also as collateral against the same client's funding needs.

STOCK LENDING

Securities are purchased by investors and then held in safekeeping, often at a custodian or Central Securities Depository (*CSD*). As part of a portfolio the securities will earn either dividend or interest and will periodically have the possibility of some kind of corporate action that affects them. Securities are also used for collateral purposes. The ability to increase or maximise the return on the securities is very important and so investors and trading houses have sought ways to utilise these assets without selling them.

To successfully achieve this, the operations function in an organisation needs to have a high degree of co-ordination and first-class communication internally and with other areas in the firm as well as with external parties. It needs to be able to monitor the securities that are being utilised, those that cannot be utilised and those that are free as well as the values of securities; and it also needs to have access to data about the liquidity in different individual types and groups of securities. In addition, the value of the securities and their precise whereabouts must be constantly available.

Managers must have a business plan for securities financing which includes the policy for stock lending and borrowing, otherwise there is a real danger that an *ad hoc* situation will be created where far from enhancing the returns on securities held, unforeseen costs and possibly losses will occur.

Stock lending is an important part of the securities settlement environment. Without the ability to borrow securities many market strategies would be impossible. Firms like market makers and those with principal trading activities or investment that entail selling short would be unable to operate. Other strategies that call for the delivery of an asset at a specific time, like a derivative going to delivery, or where there is a need for assets to use as collateral against a margin call, could not be undertaken.

Settlement risk, as was seen in Chapter 3, is very much linked with securities lending by enabling settlement of transactions to take place in a timely manner and reduce any risk of a default by the counterparty to the trade. The introduction of the central clearing counterparty (CCP) makes the availability of securities for borrowing more important as the concept of the failed trade is removed from the settlement process. In fact, the CCP is quite likely to generate a greater demand for borrowing and opportunities for lenders because of the growth of hedge funds, which utilise short selling and the needs of prime brokers to borrow securities to settle these short sales. Although netting of trades at clearing house level in the CCP does reduce the need to actually settle each sale, thereby removing the problem of waiting for securities from a bought transaction to be available, other factors – like moves to $T + 1$ or 2, reduced cross-border settlement costs, changes in market infrastructures leading to easier access to markets and greater capacity through STP – will all potentially lead to more transactions. Many of these will be short sales generating short positions, so stock lenders will still be required.

The issue of hedge funds and short sellers is an important one. Obviously, securities lending allows them to operate and the liquidity they bring to the markets is crucially important; however, there are many critics of the short sellers. In the sustained equity market falls of the summer of 2002, voices were raised condemning the activities of some hedge funds and blaming the falls on the active short selling of securities. Even if they were not directly responsible, the suggestion was that they contributed significantly to the falls making them worse than they would otherwise have been. As securities lending enables such activity it was easy to call for curbs on the lending of securities.

In the immediate aftermath of the collapse of Baring's there were similar demands for derivatives to be banned. This reaction failed to recognise the real reasons for the problem, which was of course poor management and controls, and it is a similar situation with stock lending.

Markets fall because no one wants to buy, not because people want to sell. Anyone who sells anything does so because they either do not want the item anymore or they believe that sentiment is moving into negative territory, so they speculate on selling short and buying back at lower levels. Short sellers can be aggressive in the market, but then so too can buyers and the 'shorts' can be playing a very risky game as sentiment can rapidly change and markets rally sharply. In the summer of 2002 it was the continuation of a long period of downward movement that gathered pace. Speculators borrowing stock to sell short were not the problem. The problem was that investors could see no reason to buy stock. It is all a question of value and value is affected by supply and demand (buyers versus sellers), economic and other factors (corporate scandals, growth of the US economy) and attractiveness (perceived security and the yield on equities compared with other investment vehicles). Naturally, any global issues like those concerning Iraq which was very much to the forefront of news throughout much of 2002 can have a significant impact, particularly if, as in this case, the price of oil becomes a factor.

It is sensible to consider the recommendation by the G30/ISSA shown in Box 4.1, which is far more relevant to the purpose and importance of securities lending.

Box 4.1 Recommendation No. 8 of the Group of Thirty (*G30*)

Securities lending and borrowing should be encouraged as a method of expediting the settlement of securities transactions. Existing regulatory and taxation barriers that inhibit the practice of lending and borrowing securities should be removed.

G30 (1989) updated by ISSA (1995) – visit *www.issanet.org*

Whatever the politics of it all, the operations manager must nevertheless be fully aware of the importance of securities lending and borrowing and how it impacts on their particular type of business.

Looking at securities lending, the value of an asset directly affects the lending fee that can be charged to a borrower. That value will relate to:

- availability – i.e., supply and demand;
- duration of the borrow;
- restriction on use;
- source of lending.

Securities availability will be affected by many factors, the amount of issued security being one of them. However, the amount of security in issue is different from the amount of security that could be lent. Obviously, some holders of securities have no reason, nor wish, to lend them and many cannot because of regulation, trust deed constraints or risk policies. A shortage of a security is not only prevalent in illiquid and small issues but can apply to even the largest issue and can impact in situations where a particular security is in high demand.

Examples of this include situations related to take-overs, delivery of derivatives, illiquid stocks and special stock situations like short selling.

SECURITIES LENDING PROCESS FLOWS

The process flows related to securities lending and borrowing are relatively straightforward as Figure 4.1 shows.

The compilation of procedures for this type of flow will revolve around a series of checks at the critical stages.

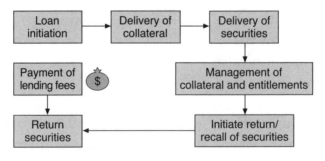

Figure 4.1 Operational work flows.
Source: the**dsc**.portfolio.

LOAN INITIATION

At loan initiation there will be credit checks on the counterparty, creation and signing of the lending agreement (including fees and collateral), and the date when the loan will commence and the duration.

DELIVERY OF COLLATERAL AND SECURITIES

There will be confirmation of the securities to be lent and the collateral to be received from the borrower. The collateral amount will be calculated based on the value of the collateral and the value of the securities lent. Instructions to deliver the securities and for receipt of the collateral will then follow. The procedures will need to determine whether this will be free of payment, delivery versus payment (in the cash collateral scenario) or delivery versus delivery.

MANAGEMENT OF BENEFITS AND COLLATERAL

During the period of the loan there is the possibility: first, that the value of the lent security and or collateral will change; second, that there may be a need to substitute alternative collateral; and, third, that there may be some kind of corporate action on either the security or the collateral or both. An example of a possible situation regarding corporate actions when cash collateral is used

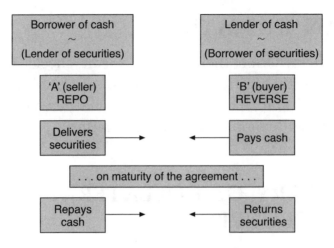

Figure 4.2 Repos – flowchart.
Source: the**dsc**.portfolio.

is given in Figure 4.2. Procedures need to be in place to ensure that this is adequately monitored and managed.

RETURN/RECALL OF SECURITIES

The lending agreement (see below) will determine the protocol for the recall/return of the securities and the release of the collateral.

PAYMENT OF FEES

The procedures for the payment of fees is started again in the lending agreement or, in the case of automated lending and borrowing via a custodian service or CSD, the fees will be debited and credited to the relevant account.

LENDING AGREEMENT

With securities lending and borrowing there are key issues, actions and requirements that must be addressed. Perhaps the most crucial is the stock lending agreement.

Before any lending or borrowing can take place the terms and conditions under which this will occur must be formalised simply because securities are being transferred usually free of payment and preferably delivery versus delivery if non-cash collateral is being used.

Central to this agreement will be the terms for the recall of the loaned security and the arrangements for collateral, including collateral substitution. Other important matters covered will include stock situations so that in the event of a takeover or merger or indeed any other corporate action, related to the lent security, both parties are quite clear on what will happen. Finally, the agreement must cover default. The London Stock Exchange has produced a Master Lending Agreement (this can be found on their website – see Useful websites and suggested further reading).

REPURCHASE AGREEMENTS (REPOS)

An alternative to securities lending and borrowing is the repurchase agreement or repo.

This involves the sale of securities and a simultaneous agreement to repurchase them at a later date. Repos are explained more fully in Chapter 5, but in effect the seller of the securities is borrowing cash against the collateral offered by the security.

Again, the principal concern for the operations manager is to ensure that the systems and procedures are able to deal with repos and the collateral issues that arise.

COLLATERAL

Collateral and collateral management is another highly important part of the operations function and the managers and supervisors play a key role in ensuring success. Collateral can be required for a variety of reasons:

- stock borrowing;
- repos;
- on-exchange derivative margin calls;
- off-exchange derivative margin calls;
- CCP margin calls; and membership capital requirements;
- loans;
- prime brokerage services.

Two key factors and two key processes occur with any collateral.

As far as key factors are concerned: first, what collateral will be acceptable and, second, will the taker of the collateral have lien over that collateral? The first may be the lender's choice, it may be governed by standard market practice or it may be dictated by regulation and in the case of, for example, a clearing house it will be their standard policy towards collateral. Lien or control over the collateral is crucial and it is here that consideration needs to be given to whether collateral is to be physically held by the lender or calling party or whether it can be pledged to them, the latter usually being a pledge form signed by the custodian holding the securities.

The two key processes are, first, the reconciliation of the collateral held against the securities lent/repoed or collateral deposited against the margin calls. The second is the valuation of the margin, securities and the collateral by mark to market. Reconciliation is critically important and to some extent dictates, in certain situations, whether collateral is needed. Therefore, the procedures for reconciliation must be robust, monitored and flexible enough to deal with the different possible situations where collateral is used. Remember this is applying to both parties and, in some circumstances, collateral can be required by both parties to a position at different times, depending on who is winning and losing.

Ensuring that sufficient collateral is held requires continuous monitoring of the value of the collateral itself and the value of the margin or security lent. The source and method of the valuation may be standard practice, like, for instance, a clearing house margining system or negotiated between the parties. In the latter there may need to be agreement on the terms of the use and deposit of the collateral. Collateral agreements can be separate documentation. Collateral is likely to be covered in a stock lending or prime brokerage agreement but, for instance, for an over-the-counter derivative trade there could be a specific collateral agreement.

Guidelines are sometimes set out for users of collateralisation processes as is the case, for example, with the ISDA 2001 *Margin Provisions*.

SECURITISATION

Securities are also used for the purpose of guaranteeing other products like bank guarantees that may be needed for clearing membership and margin cover as well as for bonds and related products that will be issued to raise capital.

It is not difficult to see that co-ordinating securities' use in various ways – to maximise returns – becomes vital to the business. The operations manager's role in this is a significant one.

Chapter

5

....

TREASURY AND FUNDING

Time is money, money is profit and loss.

Any operations function is naturally involved in the movement of money as part of the settlement processes. The movement may be payments or receipts of cash in settlement of transactions or, in some cases like derivatives, for collateral purposes. There are also various products where cash is part of the product – for instance, repurchase agreements – or associated with the product, like interest on bonds or dividends on shares.

Today, many organisations are trading globally and so cash comes in various currencies, which adds another dimension to the treasury process.

Money is constantly moving back and forth between institutions and individuals as the business of the financial markets is undertaken. It must also be remembered that money, in terms of supply and cost, is controlled by the central banks. The impact of this management by central banks feeds through into the daily and longer term treasury management process in firms involved in the financial markets. Some of the issues surrounding the cost of money to a firm when it is used in the operations function will be examined in Chapter 4 (on securities financing).

Whilst it is important for the processing and client service functions within operations to be efficient and maximise the use of cash, so too the treasury operation function needs to be efficient in dealing with the funding requirements and the excess funds available.

Generically, there is a simple enough flow related to the

Table 5.1 Accounting flow – relation to the accounting function.

Dealing	Operations	Cashiers	Accounts
Execution	Confirms Clearing Settlement Delivery	Payments Receipts	Records Documentation Management reports Reconciliations

use of cash in the firm (see Table 5.1) as this flow is part of the accounting process.

The Treasury function is primarily concerned with the management of assets and liabilities, as well as risk and relationship management. The former concerns the potential operational risks associated with, amongst other issues, payments and foreign exchange whilst the latter concerns the relationships with banks and payment systems like SWIFT.

The cash management role of the function concerns managing liquidity by utilising and servicing the cash flow and short-term assets so that funding is available in different currencies to meet the requirements of the business. As such, it is intrinsically linked to the operations function which will be both a depositor and borrower of funds to meet the settlement amounts due on a daily basis.

The treasury department in a bank is likely to be involved not only in both securities and derivatives-related funding but also other aspects of the banking function, like high-volume lending and borrowing or currency trading. As such the structure and procedures of this treasury department will be markedly different from that within a non-banking institution.

Within the treasury function several relationships are extremely important. Establishing borrowing facilities and monitoring the rates applied are crucial to effective treasury management. It is therefore usual for the re-purchase agreement (*repo*) desk in a bank and the treasury department to work closely on utilising assets and bor-rowing requirements.

After the trade and its settlement there is an environ-ment, the post-settlement environment, where the active management of the asset becomes a crucial part of the business. Funding is part of that environment and it is here that excess cash or long positions in assets are linked into this process as Figure 5.1 shows.

However, there are several processes and functions within or related to each of the three post-settlement areas shown in Figure 5.1. Figure 5.2 illustrates this.

The interaction between the funding and custody pro-cesses is considerable and, clearly, the manager needs to be certain that procedures are sufficiently robust to

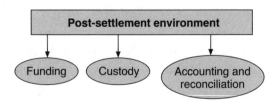

Figure 5.1   Post-settlement process areas.

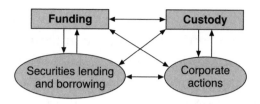

Figure 5.2   Post-settlement process areas.

ensure that the interaction works effectively and efficiently and that the risk is controlled.

One way in which the treasury implications can be better understood is to consider a transaction from execution through to settlement and post-settlement.

CASE STUDY

If a trader purchases securities, they have created a situation on settlement assuming delivery versus payment (*DVP*) of long/positive securities and short/negative cash.

The dealer has a financing cost, as, effectively, they have an overdraft and the cost of funding this position is vitally important to the final profit/loss on the trade.

The first stage in the treasury process for the trade is to be aware of the existence of the position and the value date for settlement. In many firms use is made of cash ladders or projections that incorporate all cash inflows and outflows expected each day. This enables the treasury team to assess the net requirements, analyse the assets available and also to prepare the foreign exchange transactions for different currencies.

The relevant data for this process will be sourced from settlement operations and, as there are times when the expected settlement does not take place on the due date, the data are subject to alteration. The funding process is carried out based on relative costs of borrowing or rates for deposits.

Table 5.2 shows a settlement expectation from transactions that are both current and outstanding.

What possible scenarios could occur on settlement day and what is the impact?

If it is assumed that the purchases are in fact delivered: (a) Can the sales take place? and (b) What is the funding situation?

There are problems with the overall position. Taking security ABC first, there is an old unmatched position and a depot position that is not available to be used probably as it is ring-fenced collateral. If the old unmatched/ unsettled trade is not delivered today it will be impossible to deliver the sale of 15m shares as there is a shortfall of 1.5m shares.

The settlement team should be taking steps to ensure that the delivery of the 15m shares will take place. They will try to establish whether the outstanding purchase will be delivered and also the status of the 13.5m shares due to be delivered. If there is a problem with the unmatched trade they will instigate one or more of the following:

1. A stock borrow of 1.5m shares.
2. Buy in the 16.5m shares.
3. Ask the buyer of the 15m if they will accept a partial settlement.

Table 5.2 Positions for settlement.

Purchases			Sales		
Amount (m)*	**Security**	**Value (m)***	**Amount (m)***	**Security**	**Value (m)***
10	ABC plc	6.75	15	ABC plc	13.5
3.5	ABC plc				
1	DEF plc	3	5	DEF plc	17.5
1.5	XYZ plc	2	10	XYZ	20
15	XYZ plc	22.5			
		36.25			51

Depot position			Unmatched/Settlement fails		
			Stock	**Value**	**Days**
2.5	ABC plc	N/A	Buy 7m DEF plc	17	7
			Sale 4m DEF plc	13	7
5	XYZ plc		Sale 3m DEF plc	10.5	6
			Buy 16.5m ABC plc	12	2

Projected cash position at start of settlement day

Line	15m
Available	8m

Projected dealers' positions at close of settlement day

ABC plc	Long	17.5m
DEF plc	Short	4m
XYZ plc	Long	11.5m

* 'm' stands for million, N/A for unavailable.
Source: the**dsc**.portfolio.

The exact course of events will vary depending on the market. Some more mature markets have a central clearing counterparty (CCP) structure where settlement must take place as a result of automated stock borrows and/or buy-ins. Even some markets without a CCP adopt the auto-borrow/buy-in. If the 16.5m ABC trade is actually unmatched rather than a settlement fail, then there needs to be pressure on the dealer to resolve the situation.

Other possible problems exist as well. The sale of 5m DEF shares requires the borrowing of 4m shares as the dealer is running a short position. However, there is a 7m purchase and sale outstanding which might reflect a difficult illiquid security where borrowing may not be easy, cost-effective or indeed possible. The receipt of the 10m XYZ shares is imperative if the sale is to be settled.

The issue from a treasury perspective is that if all the settlement for the day goes through there is a 14.75m inflow of cash. It is a big problem if any of the sales do not take place and purchases have to be funded. Also, there is the outstanding 16.5m shares which if it now settles will result in paying out 12m, thus reducing the positive cash flow of 14.75m to just 2.75m.

The settlement and treasury teams need to work closely together to provide the most up-to-date and accurate data on the situation. Any change must be advised immediately to enable treasury to adjust their borrowing/depositing position. At the end of the day the dealers profit and loss (p&l) will incorporate the funding costs and/or benefits, so any use of money and the security itself become crucial. Once the security is received and paid for and is in custody, what else can be done with it, assuming it has not been sold on?

In Chapter 4 (on securities financing) securities lending and borrowing as well as repos were examined. In both cases these can be utilised to generate either securities or cash. As the cash generated by repoing securities may be obtained more cheaply than borrowing from another source like the custodian or another bank, it is important that treasury have good access to money market rates and a selection of sources for both borrowing and depositing cash (see Figure 5.3). That access to money may be either on a secured or unsecured basis and both will usually be cheaper than simply running an overdraft at the custodian.

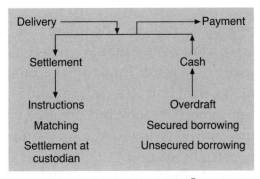

Figure 5.3 Borrowing flow.

The cost of borrowing even short term can vary, so monitoring the market rates is a key part of the treasury function. When the treasury team need to borrow funds they will execute either an unsecured borrowing trade or a secured borrowing trade like a repo.

Treasury therefore has its own transactions to settle, and procedures will need to be documented for this as well as the financing relationship it has with operations.

UNSECURED BORROWING

Details for an unsecured trade will include:

- trade time and date;
- type (borrowing or receipt of cash/loan or payment of cash);
- currency;
- amount;
- counterparty;
- opening value date;
- closing value date;
- interest rate.

The other procedures that will be important include the possible issue of a pre-advice which enables the receiving bank/custodian to position funds in the money market on value date. If a firm borrows cash to fund the overdraft created by a purchase of stock but no advice is issued, a custodian may not be aware of the incoming cash until the funds are actually received and may not then be in a position to place that money. The result will be that the account is not credited with the amount and one extra day of interest on the overdraft accrues as well as the interest on the borrowing.

When a borrowing is repaid, an instruction or wire transfer is made that includes the amount borrowed plus the interest that has accrued. If the closing value date is missed, penal rates of interest may be charged to the borrower by the lender.

SECURED BORROWING

Secured borrowing is where collateral is offered whilst the cash is borrowed and, as the risk to the lender is reduced, the cost of borrowing is usually lower. Repos are a common form of secured borrowing where a security is used as collateral, hence the reason why it is sometimes referred to as collateralised borrowing.

The following example is based on one given in the excellent *Mastering Repo Markets* by Rob Steiner (published by FT/Pitman).

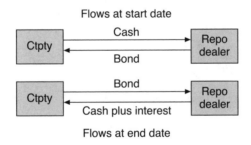

Figure 5.4   Classic repos.
Source: the**dsc**.portfolio.

Box 5.1 Repo detail.	
Deal date:	15/07/02
Settlement date:	17/07/02
Term:	28 days (14/08/02)
Repo rate:	4% (ACT/360 basis)
Collateral:	60m nominal 8.5% bond with maturity 26th March 2004

Source: the**dsc**.portfolio.

Box 5.2   Repo

Value of collateral:

$$\text{Clean price} = 108.95$$

$$\text{Accrued coupon} = \frac{111}{360} \times 8.5\%$$

$$= 2.620\,833\,33$$

$$\text{Total purchase price} = 111.570\,833\,33$$

$$\text{Total purchase amount} = 60m \times \frac{111.570\,833\,33}{100}$$

$$= 66{,}942{,}500.00$$

Source: the**dsc**.portfolio.

Box 5.3   Repo

On maturity of the repo, the seller will repay the cash with interest calculated at 4%:

$$\text{Principal} = 66{,}942{,}500$$

$$\text{Interest} = 66{,}942{,}500 \times 0.04 \times \frac{28}{360}$$

$$= 208{,}256.56$$

Source: the**dsc**.portfolio.

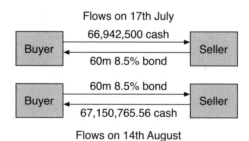

Flows on 17th July

Flows on 14th August

Figure 5.5   Repo flows.

Source: the**dsc**.portfolio.

Figures 5.1–5.5 show the flow for a repo, and basically both parties benefit. The repo desk has secured the required cash against the 60m bond and repays the cash plus the interest at 4%. The lender of the cash has the bond as security and could lend that bond on and earn further income.

The operations manager dealing with these types of trades must be aware of possible events whilst the repo is in place. Rate changes affect open repos, collateral substitution may be required and a coupon may be paid.

The classic repo is one where either the trade is on a term basis, where the closing value date is agreed and therefore everything including the interest rate is fixed, or open basis, where the closing value date is not yet agreed and will not be until one of the parties needs to close it, whereupon the closing value date will be agreed. As mentioned above, the repo rate can change with an open repo.

Repos are either made between two parties, otherwise known as 'bilateral trading' or if one party uses an agent it is known as a 'tri-party' repo. Various parties will undertake the agent role including the two ICSDs, Euroclear and Clearstream.

Money market instruments

Various instruments are available in the money markets to enable short-term deposits or borrowings. These include:

- certificates of deposit;
- bills of exchange;
- commercial paper.

Derivatives

There are also various derivatives that are used in managing money such as:

- short-term interest rate futures and options;
- interest rate swaps;
- currency futures and options;
- currency forwards;
- currency swaps;
- forward rate agreements.

Foreign exchange

The main foreign exchange (*FX*) deals will be spot, forward, currency options and currency swaps. Deals are transacted by telephone or, increasingly, on dealing systems, and London is the main centre for FX dealing. Transactions in FX are for:

- use of the currency – e.g., the holiday maker;
- hedging;
- speculation.

A list of suggested reading is provided on p. 313 for readers wanting to understand more about these products.

Treasury settlements

The operations team responsible for treasury settlements is supporting the trading activities of the bank and the funding activities associated with various parts of the firm. As with all operations functions the automation of processes has reduced the time available to verify transactions and resolve any problems. The processes undertaken in treasury settlements are important because they feed data into p&l, risk management and financial control. Errors, therefore, have a major impact because incorrect funding is usually expensive.

Box 5.4   Functions of the Treasury Settlement Area.

1. Support dealing activities.
2. Control risks.
3. Process transactions.
4. Record transactions in accounting system.
5. Cash transfers and cash management.
6. Validation of data by day end.
7. Meet deadlines for processing and information generation.

Source: the**dsc**.portfolio.

Many features of treasury settlement are similar to those for securities:

- deal capture;
- deal verification;
- settlement instructions;
- confirmations;
- payments;
- reconciliation.

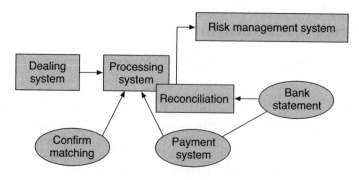

Figure 5.6 System-generated flows.

Treasury settlement is becoming increasingly automated and straight-through-processing (*STP*) is evident. In an STP environment there are:

- deal capture;
- standard settlement instructions.

The systems create a situation similar to that shown in Figure 5.6.

Some types of instrument cannot be incorporated into an STP environment – such as bills of exchange – as a signature is required on the physical bill.

Cash management

The end product of the treasury department's processes is the effective management of the movement of cash. Cash moves via payment systems, and when a firm is trading internationally it will often appoint an agent or agents to undertake this role for the payment systems in different markets and countries. These agents are commonly referred to as *correspondent banks*. The account that is operated for the firm by the agent is called a *nostro*[1] account (the agent calls it a *vostro* account).

The process requires good communication between the firm and the correspondent bank as there may well be many instructions, numerous amounts being credited and debited to the firm's nostro account and potentially plenty of operational risk. Details of movements must be reconciled, so the provision of statements in a timely manner can be crucial. Often, the correspondent bank is also used by the treasury dealers and this can be of benefit when the official cut-off time for payment has passed, as a rectifying deal with the correspondent bank can be made and a book transfer settlement made.

There are several payment systems that are operated for different types of business including large-value funds transfer systems (LVFTS) such as Clearing House Inter-bank Payment System (CHIPS) in the US and Clearing House Automated Payment System (CHAPS) in the UK. As one would expect, netting and real time gross settlement are issues in treasury settlement in much the same way as they are in the settlement of securities.

As has already been noted, cash ladders or forecasting is crucial to effective and efficient cash management. Accurate and timely messages are needed for instructions, confirms and payments. Organisations like SWIFT become key to that process and the reader, if they are not

---

[1] From the Italian for 'our' and *vostro* for 'your'.

familiar with SWIFT, should visit their website (see p. 313) for an overview of the organisation.

Risk in treasury settlement

Finally in this chapter, the risk situations that the operations manager must deal with need to be considered. Market and credit risk obviously apply to treasury dealing and counterparties. Many transactions are over the counter (*OTC*). However, the advent of facilities like RepoClear and CLS in the foreign exchange market, details of both of which are available on their websites (see p. 313), is reducing some counterparty risks.

Settlement risk in treasury settlement is about the timing of payments. A payment that is termed 'irrevocable' means that the payment has been issued and cannot be cancelled unilaterally. Funds are received with finality when the domestic payment system has completed its procedures and funds credited to the account cannot be reversed. In principle, the risk status moves from low – i.e., a payment has not been issued and can be cancelled – to high – i.e., the payment cannot be cancelled but the purchased amount has not been confirmed with finality.

In other respects, operational risk issues are the same as those for other types of settlement so we have risks associated with:

- processes;
- systems;
- data integrity;

- communication;
- security;
- people.

There is also of course regulation involved as well as agreements, so both regulatory and legal risk exist.

For the operations manager the relationship between securities and treasury settlement must be maintained at the highest standard and a full understanding of the respective roles by both teams is highly desirable. Like-wise, it is important that the technology teams servicing the two settlement areas understand the interaction between the two.

Without good procedures and efficient systems too much time will be spent on dealing with settlement and payment fails, incorrect funding and inefficient use of money.

Operations managers should never forget:

Time is money, money is profit and loss.

Chapter

6

. . . .

RESOURCE MANAGEMENT

If you can keep your head when all about you are losing theirs ...

Rudyard Kipling

The successful management of resource is an obvious requirement in any organisation. Adequate resource levels are vitally important in not only managing efficiency but also risk. However, achieving successful resource management in an operations function presents several unique problems.

These problems do not affect just operations teams in financial market organisations. Similar problems can occur in, for example, the health service and the teaching profession. A more accurate description might be a common problem that may be compounded by occurring in a financial markets environment or be specific to an operations team rather than another part of the firm.

However you look at it, resource management is a key issue.

PRESSURES ON RESOURCE

Workflow can generate problems. Erratic volumes of business, long hours and critical deadlines all put pressure on resource.

To analyse the impact of the processes and procedures on the operation workflow needs to be examined.

It is important to be able to measure the impact of workflow. The breaking down of functions, actions, events and deadlines show how the flow through the section or sections in operations occurs. The resource available can be applied to this analysis. Thus, it can be ascertained what resource is needed, what is available and how that resource can be efficiently utilised, given the workflow.

The application of resource to task or tasks is only part of resource management. There are other key elements, such as development of individuals and teams as well as identifying the skill sets needed and, remembering that operations is a business, the commercially viable level of resource that is likely to be available.

To enable the full picture of resource against workflow we can again turn to the workflow charts and this time extrapolate the key and secondary functions and the frequency and duration of processes. Having done this we will now have knowledge of when and where the workload is heaviest, where and when we have resource available, how that resource can be assigned to tasks to provide for maximum efficiency and minimised risk. At every stage in this process we come back to what resource is available, so that understanding the skills of the team and the individuals and recognising the constraints that might exist in terms of systems, employment law, head-count and budgetary considerations becomes an essential part of the manager's role.

Categorising people and their attributes is not a straight-forward process.

There may be expertise. But, at what level is that expertise when compared with a competing organisation? For instance, a manager in a medium-size bank/fund manager which decides to start using a new product, such as futures and options, would need to consider what they and the team know about derivatives.

Depending on the answer, which hopefully will be that they know something about specific parts of the derivative industry, the perceived expertise level of the operations team will have changed from good to excellent for the existing business to maybe adequate to good for the new derivatives product.

The point is that bland analysis of the skill sets of individuals is no use whatsoever. Actual skill levels need to be capable of measurement – including product awareness which must encompass all main financial markets and instruments, whether or not they are currently traded by the firm or its clients – and the skills need to be applied to tasks set out in the procedures.

Ask yourself how much you know about each member of your team. Would you know which team members have passed recognised industry examinations without referring to records from the personnel department? Do you personally oversee their training and are you fully involved in their appraisals? Would you be aware if a team member was undertaking additional training and examinations in their own time? Do you know how many of the team understand derivatives or foreign exchange or speak a language or are qualified in first aid?

The manager must develop skills in the team, and to do that needs to be able to define the skill set requirements for each task. All too often there is a surfeit of certain skills and a chronic need for other skills. The result is that performance is impaired and inconsistent.

There is no escaping the fact that poor resource management causes this situation. So, how do you ensure that you manage resource efficiently and effectively?

To start with you need to undertake an exercise with relevant people in your team. Box 6.1 is an illustration of the kind of exercise that might be suitable.

Box 6.1 Skills exercise.	
Question 1:	What are the skill sets needed for your current business and operations function?
Question 2:	What skill sets does your resource currently possess?
Question 3:	What additional skill sets are essential to obtain and which would be advantageous but are currently not critical?
Question 4:	How do I go about achieving the level of skills I need?

Source: the**dsc**.portfolio.

This is not a small undertaking. To help with the process you can utilise skill set templates such as the one shown in Table 6.1.

There can be little doubt that most managers view resource management as a primary, key core role.

Table 6.1   Operations skills template.

Business induction	Regulation
Trading and dealing	Money laundering
Operations	FSA
Administration	International regulation
Understanding the risk culture	Role of compliance

Product	Personal skills
Role of financial markets	Communications
Specific products	Languages
Equity	Dealing with business areas
Bond	Dealing with clients
Money markets	Telephone manner
Derivatives	Report writing
Clearing and settlement	Using technology
Treasury	Systems
Client services	Software
	Email
	Teamwork

Qualifications
  Business-related competency
  Regulatory

DEFINING RESOURCE

Resource is the infrastructure that supports the business of operations. It is therefore related to the technology and human aspects of the operations function.

Both the human and technology resource may be provided by external parties, and in the latter case this can apply to both systems and information technology (*IT*) staff. The outsourcing of some or all of the technology support for a business is not uncommon. Neither is the outsourcing of all or part of the operations function (this will be considered later). The operations manager might therefore have to manage both permanent employees of the company and, indirectly, employees of another organisation. This can be difficult in terms of creating team spirit, but, equally, is beneficial to the firm as it enables flexibility in a crucially important function by enabling resource to be employed on a project basis rather than being part of permanent headcount.

In the globalised industry which exists today there are therefore resource issues that encompass not only people and systems but also procedures, processes and regulatory or legal requirements. The scope of the manager's role can vary markedly between firms and organisations and is often heavily dependent on the geographical location and the organisational structure of the business. Managing central resource and resource issues can be shared between several managers whilst managing specific resource is more likely to be vested in a single manager. For instance, the training and development of personnel is likely to be managed by both a centralised HR area and the managers of individual areas. This is an important issue as communication and clear objectives are needed if individual staff members and the business are not to suffer from lack of adequate training.

TRAINING AND DEVELOPING PEOPLE

Clearly, the training and development of people is crucial to most businesses and, yet, often the process becomes confused and not entirely successful because of the shared responsibility.

The manager's role in developing people is likely to be driven by:

- contingency planning;
- skill sets within the team or teams;
- business lines and services;
- regulatory requirements;
- individuals' career objectives.

Each of these needs careful assessment.

CONTINGENCY PLANNING

What is the 'people plan'?

A supplementary question is 'should we recruit or develop'?

A manager must have a very clear idea of what is expected of people individually and as part of a team. The essential recognition is that the performance, qualities and skills of a team will not grow uniformly or even stay the same. Even when a manager inherits a strong team, there needs to be continuous appraisal and reappraisal of the merits of each person and the collective merit of the team. A successful team is not naturally born. It is created and maintained by skilled management. It is created by the selection of people and maintained by the development of those people. Successful teams, once created, do not remain successful without constant enhancement, so the manager must manage.

When looking to create the team a manager is conscious of the need to maintain the same consistency in quality and performance. It is a difficult task for several reasons, not least that available budget/headcount will go some way to determining the extent of cover that can be arranged for skills and people. However, one of the most important questions for the manager is what will change in the processes and procedures that the team undertake which will significantly alter the skills and/or headcount?

The people plan is certainly about contingency because maintaining both quality and performance requires the manager to consider changing the skill sets and the head-count and, therefore, the team. A good manager will pre-empt this by building into the planning process the re-engineering of the workforce. This concept is the same for any team and examples abound in, for instance, team sports and political (government) teams. However, these examples are also where there can be high levels of success for a period, sometimes a substantial period (the Thatcher government) followed by a far less success-ful period.

In the financial services industry there are some parallels that can be drawn:

• The London International Financial Futures Exchange (*LIFFE*) board and team had a huge success story that abruptly halted when it failed to foresee and then respond quickly to the threat posed by the then Deutsche Terminbörse.

- Andersen's team had built a highly successful audit business that floundered on the rock that was Enron.
- The numerous highly successful dotcom management teams that created a bandwagon of rapid growth companies, most of which failed to maintain the growth and subsequently collapsed.

The operations manager needs to be wary of creating something successful and assuming it will automatically continue.

Looking at the structure of the operations team there are several key industry initiatives that are without question changing the way in which operations, and therefore operations teams, work. These include:

- straight through processing (*STP*);
- central clearing counterparties (*CCP*);
- electronic markets/settlement;
- Basel/risk management requirements and policies;
- new and enhanced technology to meet globalised trading and the increasing sophistication of clients;
- adoption of G30/ISSA recommendations on:
  - ○ shortening settlement cycles;
  - ○ dematerialised settlement.

Each of these is having the effect of changing the role of the operations person from a processor to a risk manager and provider of client facing services. This requires re-engineering throughout the operations function and is a significant resource management project for the operations manager.

Issues that will need to be addressed include:

- identifying the restructuring needs;
- development and implementation;
- the timetable for change;
- re-training;
- recruitment.

RESTRUCTURING

The major technology projects like STP are creating an entirely new processing environment and obviously one that needs, on the face of it, less human intervention. As a result the previous procedures and processes will need reviewing and updating and personnel will:

1. Become obsolete as the specific job specification disappears or is significantly amended.
2. Require retraining to be able to work with new procedures or to undertake an entirely new function.
3. Require replacement as the individual is not capable of or has no interest in undertaking a new role.

Each of these options will depend on the person and the exact role they performed and are required to perform in the future. To some extent it will also depend on the other resource that is available as very often the impact of technology advancements or changes to working practices result in a situation where there are two or three people when only one is needed.

The issue now for the manager is not as simple as choice, although that in itself can be a very hard decision. It is also about the reaction of the team to the decision that the manager takes and the impact that this has on morale.

When a team is fortunate enough to possess many top-quality people the enforced loss of those people can be very difficult for the manager and the colleagues of the individuals concerned. There is, by and large, a natural solidarity amongst teams of people, so the instinct is to expect the managers to somehow retain these colleagues. Perversely, if the manager takes a soft option and artificially creates a position this can be just as big a blow to morale as announcing redundancies. The manager may opt for this course, as there is a belief and usually a hope that the situation is only temporary and that a permanent position can be found; however, a false job will end up creating resentment and do nothing for the person concerned, however well meant the action may have been. Unless there is unequivocal evidence that a position will become available that the individual is suited for, the manager owes it to that person and the team not to create an artificial position.

Most organisations today will have extensive support for anyone unfortunate enough to be made redundant. In reality it doesn't make it any less painful, but at least there is some effort to minimise the impact. That hasn't always been the case and may still not be in smaller organisations.

TRAINING AND PERSONAL DEVELOPMENT

Successful resource management demands effective training at all levels.

What constitutes effective training?

- Identifying the strengths and weaknesses in individuals.
- Developing skills to meet current and future developments.
- Succession planning.
- Identifying and implementing training programs.
- Devising collective awareness programs covering such areas as customer service and risk.
- Keeping training logs.
- Continuous Personnel Development (*CPD*) for **all** the team.

Managing the development of the team is going to be time-consuming but the pay-off is considerable and the consequences of not doing it potentially dire.

What are the risks of not managing training?

1. Inability of individuals to handle tasks.
2. Inability of team to handle multiple or connected tasks.

3. Reduction in quality of work.
4. Failure to maintain adequate service levels.
5. Loss of image.
6. Increased operational risk.
7. Higher costs through inefficiency and error.
8. Dissatisfied staff.
9. Failure to retain quality staff.
10. Poor productivity.
11. Knock-on effect in the organisation.
12. Regulatory risk (i.e., training and competency regime).

All are evidence of some degree of failure to manage training and development. The consequences may be immediate – e.g., loss of staff – or may become apparent over time – e.g., loss of clients, increasing numbers of errors, etc.

There are pointers available to management from the workflow analysis. The following two exercises give an illustration of how to go about this.

Box 6.2 Exercise 1.

Consider and list the ways in which workflow charts and analysis can highlight training-related issues.

Box 6.3 Exercise 2.

What specific training requirements are there for derivative operations personnel?

Once these tasks have been completed the picture will be clearer about what is needed to make the function operate efficiently. To assist with the second exercise a training and development planner can be used (Table 6.2).

SUCCESSION PLANNING

Part of resource management is succession planning.

Long gone are the days when a team of people would stay together at the same employer for almost the whole of their careers. Today the successful resource manager is one who recognises that things will change, not just in terms of work practices and processes but also personnel.

Too often time and money is spent developing individuals and teams to a point of excellence only for one or more key personnel to then leave within a short time.

The effect on the remaining team members can be mixed. Some will see opportunity, others will see the downside. The lead given by managers and supervisors at this time will be crucial. People will want to see the game plan, be reassured and maybe realise ambitions.

Failure to manage this successfully will cause immediate and longer-term problems as the third exercise (Box 6.4) shows by illustrating the kinds of issue that needs addressing.

Table 6.2 Operations skills template – operations personnel development plan.

Within 6 months	
Business induction	*Regulation*
Trading and dealing	Money laundering
Operations	
Administration	
Understanding the risk culture	

Within 2 years	
Product	*Personal skills*
Role of financial markets	Communications
Specific products	Languages
Equity	Dealing with business areas
Bond	Dealing with clients
Money markets	Telephone usage
Derivatives	Report writing
Clearing and settlement	Using technology
Treasury	Systems
Client services	Software
	Email
Regulation	Teamwork
Regulatory environment	Meetings
Role of domestic regulator	Presentations
International regulation	
Role of compliance	

Within 5 years	
Qualifications	*Personal skills*
Second level business-related competency	Supervisor's role
Second level regulatory	Manager's role

Source: the**dsc**.portfolio.

> *Box 6.4* Exercise 3.
>
> Consider an operations team that loses a key member of the client service team and the No. 2 on the reconciliations team. Who is affected, in what way and what steps must be taken to manage this successfully?

DEALING WITH PEOPLE

Part of the manager's role is to deal with people in key situations. Some of these will be related to the day-to-day performance and business of the operations team. Much of the day-to-day relationship is however managed by the supervisors and team or section leaders.

The manager must deal with their staff both on a personal basis and clearly with corporate objectives in mind. It is not always a happy marriage. In the operations team of today there is change and the mindset of employees has long since dismissed company loyalty as a quaint historical phenomenon. Today the employee is more independent-minded, professional and views their place within the industry as potentially a phase in a career rather than the career. There are of course many employees in more junior roles who have more pressing short-term objectives related to earnings rather than any set career plan.

In the wider scheme of things there is still competition from firms seeking to add skills and sometimes critical mass to the operations team, and of course individuals are more than happy to move from one firm to another for more money and/or better prospects. Therefore, the working environment, reputation of the firm and the managers, and profitability all become a crucial consideration in the mind of quality people.

The manager must be aware of this wider picture and respond to the need to focus on what makes the person motivated, what they can offer the manager and what the firm and their specific area look like from the outside.

In a similar vein the manager must be prepared for the problem of matching reality to expectation.

This is not solely about remuneration; it can be, and often is these days, about the working environment. The tragic events of September 11th have changed the perception of the workplace. Quality time is now the vogue and any decent manager has realised this to be crucial. Flexibility of working hours, location and levels of pressure/stress are key components in the working environment. Some of these issues are outside the operations manager's domain but, nevertheless, the need to keep these items high on the agenda within the firm is the responsibility of the operations manager in conjunction with human resources and the business management, and many require the manager's action.

In managing the people in the team the manager must look at three separate and yet collectively important issues:

1. Remuneration of the employee.
2. Training and development.
3. Working environment.

These three can become complex, and it is also likely that the manager will need to create some elements of trade-off across all three to remain within budgets set by the business. How well this is managed will have a profound effect on the individual and the team as a whole. It is not a case either of managing this on a once a year basis as the judgement day, otherwise often known as 'appraisal day', comes around. No manager in their right mind can treat their employees with contempt and expect to get respect or performance as a result, and yet the whole process of annual appraisals is potentially flawed.

Far better is the quarterly review. It may be time-consuming in a business where time is not a commodity that exists in abundance, but it does create a much clearer and relevant situation for the individual and is much more productive for the management.

Issues that would otherwise surface only after they have become entrenched in the individual's mind can be discussed and dealt with long before they become a problem. Empowering the individual by seeking their views and showing genuine desire to ensure that high levels of communication and trust exists between the manager/supervisor and staff member can only produce beneficial results. Managers must make time and not hide behind time as an excuse.

There are numerous issues about managing people and, as the training template showed, the manager learning communication and people management skills is crucial.

What about other resource?

THE WORKING ENVIRONMENT

In any kind of work, it is not much fun or satisfying to work day in day out with poor equipment, be it the building, the furniture, the technology or even the ease of access to the workplace. The operations manager must take responsibility for seeking the best possible working environment and part of that process is to manage technology effectively.

Technology is at the heart of all operations business and poor technology in terms of both infrastructure and people skills will inevitably lead to inefficient performance and of course resentment within the team at having their own performance compromised. *Managing Technology in the Operations Function* is the subject of a Securities Institute/Butterworth-Heinemann book and the reader may want to obtain a copy.

MANAGING SYSTEMS

Systems are crucial to operations. The effectiveness of systems depends on both the suitability of the system for the business being undertaken and the capability of managers and supervisors to utilise the system.

It is also essential that the systems are recognised as key risk components being vulnerable to both failure and security risk.

The interaction between people and systems is at the heart of the operation.

Links to various sources of information as well as users accessing the systems will be a key factor in the effectiveness and efficiency of the operation in general and impacts significantly in areas such as:

- client facing products and services;
- group risk management;
- STP.

The robustness of systems is a key regulatory requirement and is also a key internal risk matter.

One only needs to look at cases where system failures have precipitated dire consequences for organisations. Brokerage businesses have ceased functioning because of the inability to meet the regulatory competency levels for settlement of transactions. Failures in control over static data, system access, and input and amendment of data have generated high-profile 'disasters'.

Consider the following extract from the *Futures and Options Association Guidelines for End-users of Derivatives* which was published in 1995 and updated in 2004 (visit *www.foa.co.uk*), yet still a fundamental concept today:

Systems approval

Computer systems used for recording derivatives transactions should be subject to the same procedures and controls as other systems used by the organisation (including contingency plans and back-up). In particular, the pricing models and trade recording systems should be properly controlled to ensure that only authorised amendments or overrides are made. Systems should be reviewed to ensure that they integrate properly into the organisation's normal reporting systems, that they are sufficiently robust to be able to continue to operate as the number of transactions increases and that they comply with any applicable regulatory requirements.

Figure 6.1 shows some of the generic links between systems. It is obvious that many processes and instructions move between these systems every day. All these data are critical and the robustness factor means that no weak link can exist in the chain without serious implications for quality, reliability and risk control.

Given this importance of the systems, which cannot be overemphasised, there are significant questions for

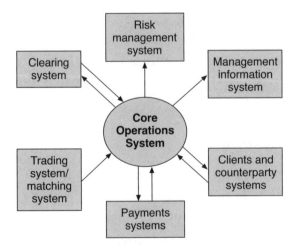

Figure 6.1   Generic links.

managers to answer:

- What are the objectives for the systems employed?
- How is the effectiveness of systems measured?
- What are the resource and skill sets needed for support?
- What are the contingency plans that are needed against failures?
- What level and type of security policy is needed for the systems?
- What are the benefits and disadvantages of the systems used?
- What integration and interaction with other internal/ external systems will occur?

Each of these questions must be answered if managers and supervisors are to be in control of the systems used in the operations area. Without answers to these questions a benchmarking exercise cannot be undertaken.

In measuring the system performance, differentiation between technical performance and operational performance is needed.

TECHNICAL PERFORMANCE

The system supplier and operating platform used will normally be decided by the central IT function. Operations managers will naturally be involved in the deliberations.

The IT department will decide whether the system is performing to the specifications required and will update, upgrade and maintain the systems as appropriate.

OPERATIONAL PERFORMANCE

This involves the operations managers and supervisors monitoring the performance of the system in relation to the original objectives.

Technical issues will come into this process as system downtime will be logged and raised with the technical support team.

Other performance issues will be the ability of the system to:

- generate the data in the required format;
- produce data in timely manner;
- handle products;
- complete functions such as margin and revaluation;
- interface with other systems.

To be able to undertake this performance monitoring requirement, data will be required from:

- the system itself;
- users via valuation.

In both cases, logs need to be maintained and received. These data must then be analysed to provide a continuous profile of the system from both technical and operational viewpoints.

The analysis will concentrate on the impact of the system's performance on the workflow.

The combination of the data and analysis of impact will

permit the managers to monitor developments of new software and/or upgrading and replacement of systems.

As changes, and in particular a switch to a new system, is not something that can be achieved overnight, the monitoring of system performance, and its impact, is vitally important.

In terms of contingency planning, without a clear understanding of the system's role and the duration of each task in the process, the processes in the event of any kind of system failure or problem cannot be prioritised.

Security over data on systems is also a key issue. Logging on to the system needs to be monitored and verified as authorised. Password discipline needs to be enforced through education about its importance and the control that it provides.

The following exercise (Box 6.5) would be a prudent one for a manager and his team to undertake:

Box 6.5   Exercise 4.
What should system performance monitoring by managers and supervisors include, what is the source of the data and how should it be used?

DIFFICULT PEOPLE

Relationships at all levels, internal and external, are so fundamentally important in the industry that a manager

unable to communicate and build good working relationships is going to struggle badly. This is a crucial issue
for the manager. Part of management training should
cover this area and the coaching the manager receives
needs to be passed on to the supervisors and team leaders.

Not all situations can be dealt with by the manager and
good communication between human resources and
managers is vital. One thing that is certain is that the
manager must know when and when not to intervene,
otherwise the status of the supervisor can be under-
mined. Equally, the manager must be prepared to be
frank and open in any discussion, show no prejudice
and above all be consistent in dealing with issues that
may arise.

The performance of people is driven by their own motivation and that provided by their supervisors and managers.

Measuring that performance is essential but is also
potentially one of the most difficult tasks performed
by the manager/supervisor.

Traditional forms of performance measurement such as
appraisals have merit providing they are done well. If they
are not done well the outcome is usually a major disaster.

Most people believe they are doing well, some believe
they are performing impressively. To be told otherwise
is not easy to take, even when deep down the person
concerned knows the facts to be true.

It is important to be aware that the supervisor and

manager have very different roles in the team. Both are motivators and organisers (in different ways) and both sit in judgement on the individuals and the team.

That judgement and the individual's expectations are frequently at odds with each other and, as a result, relationships, performance (individual and the team) and working environment can dramatically change for the worse.

How is this problem overcome?

The manager and supervisors must work out a policy towards staff that is:

- motivating;
- credible;
- implemented;
- capable of scrutiny;
- within the HR policy in the organisation;
- within the law.

MOTIVATION

Motivation comes in various forms. There is financial inducement, career advancement through promotional promises, profit share, ranking or grade, travel and perks.

Real motivation is a mixture of recognition and reward. Reward does not have to be financial or even promotion-based.

Reward means little at the end of the day if it is not justified. Reward must be fair and, therefore, the basis for reward must be flexible and not narrow. However, at the heart of it all is the recognition skill shown by managers and supervisors.

This recognition skill constitutes:

- understanding of the processes and procedures being undertaken;
- the role of individuals in these processes and procedures;
- the measurement of performance;
- the impact and influence of external relationships and counterparts;
- an understanding of the individual as a person;
- identifying, acknowledging and resolving problems;
- involving people in decisions and information;
- even-handed treatment and consistent policy of and towards issues and people;
- respecting people and their efforts.

People need to have respect for colleagues in order to be motivated and this is true at all levels. An example is a football team. If certain players are not performing and results go against the team, confidence is lost, respect for the coach begins to fade and the results get even worse.

Managers and supervisors earn respect because they demonstrate the ability to look and listen, to see problems and offer solutions, to take action and not sit on the fence, to be critical but fair.

Respect for the managers leads to motivation. Creating a

motivational environment is important but there are pitfalls such as:

- overrewarding someone;
- underrewarding someone;
- overpromoting;
- underpromoting;
- promising solutions that are not delivered;
- overcriticising;
- underreprimanding.

For most managers these are the headline issues which they will confront as they respond to different situations in the operation.

Each of them presents the likelihood of an undermining of the manager/supervisor's respect in the minds of individuals and, usually, the team.

Worse still, these views may not be stated or obvious but the damage is nevertheless happening.

Many a manager has been of the opinion that they manage their people superbly whilst the opposite view is taken by their staff. Sooner or later the problems will surface and by then it is too late. Managers and supervisors must take time to understand motivation and to reflect on the importance of issues to staff, even when the manager cannot see why it should be important. Communication, listening and accepting that others may have ideas that are worthy of consideration, and being seen to take action and above all explain the reasons for the action, are vital.

NO MOTIVATION MEANS TROUBLE IS BREWING

The pitfalls that await the manager/supervisor are many. People are fickle and have great expectations far above what is achievable or can be given.

Consider Table 6.3, where the risks associated with fairly routine manager/supervisor day-to-day work are highlighted.

PERFORMANCE MEASUREMENT

Managers and supervisors will have a feel for how their team is performing, and that feel is an essential benchmark. However, there needs to be more substance to the analysis of performance and this takes the form of comparisons, tracking and adjustments to procedures. Analysis of workflow – through the use of workflow charts, for instance – will achieve two things:

- provide the data needed to make any adjustment to structure and/or procedures;
- show team members that management is aware of the current and potential future situations.

Accurate management information on the performance of individuals, the team, the procedures and the controls is vital for any realistic and, therefore, meaningful assessments to be made. There is a danger that staff will interpret workflow analysis as having hidden agendas like headcount reduction. Adequate involvement and

Table 6.3

Situation	Info/action/ origin	Manager	Staff member/ team	Risk
Salary review	Appraisal	Works within budget	Has expectations	High risk potential of demotivation
New grade/ recruitment	Appraisal/ business growth/ leavers	Works within headcount	Expect resolution, but are concerned that new promotion/ entrant does not affect their own prospects	High risk potential of demotivation
Falling standards/ performance	MI*/ feedback/ complaints/ growth in volumes, shortage of staff	Works within budget constraints	Expect resolution. Do not accept/ understand business issues	Potential for dissatisfaction and negative reaction to any criticism
Personality clash	Feedback observation	HR considerations	Expect resolution. Probably two 'camps' supporting the individuals	Risk of appearing to support one or other protagonists. Demotivating for the losing camp
Poor performer	Feedback appraisals	Must act	Team await the decision (may or may not have sympathy with individual)	Over- or underreaction will both be badly received and demotivate

* MI stands for 'management information'.

communication will overcome this, particularly if the positive outcome of the process is explained.

Workflow analysis in generic terms provides data on:

- What is being processed and when?
- How it is impacted by factors such as volume?
- What resource is available?
- Where do pressure points occur?
- Where do problems occur?
- What scope is there for change?

By analysing the primary, secondary and periodic processes and tasks, their expected and actual duration, and whether the resource is being optimised, managers can judge the performance level.

They can also plan ahead, introduce change and have information to support their argument for change. These charts are simple to produce and maintain and provide credible support information essential to the day-to-day and long-term management of the operations team.

MANAGEMENT OF PEOPLE

To put this whole subject into perspective, how the issues outlined above interact needs to be considered. Suitable external benchmarks also need to be considered. Figure 6.2 gives some ideas on this subject.

Figure 6.2 attempts to show how the source of informa-

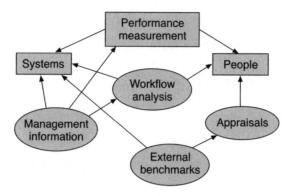

Figure 6.2 Information source and flow.
Source: the dsc.portfolio.

tion is utilised to provide various viewpoints on the assessment of systems and people.

This will enable managers to make informed decisions on everything from salaries and grades to system enhancement and procedure changes. In many cases the information is routinely available; in others it may need research (e.g., external benchmarks).

Once it is obtained a whole range of options are available, all of which help in the managing of people and system processes.

A few examples would be:

- training requirements;
- system enhancements;
- automation;
- better working environment;
- contingency planning;
- business planning;
- motivation.

The management of people and systems is a key function of managers and supervisors. To recap, the objectives are:

- risk management;
- efficiency;
- cost-effectiveness;
- competitive advantage;
- developing and implementing procedures;
- control;
- compliance with regulation and controls;
- business development;
- continuity and development of staff;
- provision of client services;
- record keeping.

The demands on managers and supervisors are considerable. Today, the role has been expanded and, as well as operational issues such as processes and procedures, we now have skills requirements in the client facing and risk management areas. We can also add to this an involvement in profit generation and protection.

With such a change in the role and a situation where significant change is also occurring in the industry in all sorts of ways, the manager's role in ensuring that systems are capable of handling the current and future business and that the team is being trained and retrained to meet the new environment is, to say the least, demanding.

Communication and awareness are essential, respect must be earned and that can only be achieved with adequate information gleaned from sources such as appraisals, management information, workflow charts and, above all, talking to people. Managing people and systems needs personal as well as technical skills, leadership and motivation in order to achieve the goal.

Underestimating the complexity of the task would be foolish as good managers are created not born.

Chapter

7

....

TECHNOLOGY IN OPERATIONS

Technology is both power and danger.

David Loader and Graeme Biggs

W hatever else the manager needs, an understanding of what accounting is and how technology works is absolutely critical. But what really are the technology issues for operations managers?

Leaving aside the fundamentals – like adequate, reliable systems – technology issues amount to the ability to manage the technology requirement and the ability to manage the use of the technology so that it generates the cost-effective and risk-managed operations function that is required.

Technology is not cheap and neither is it the panacea to all the problems that occur in operations. In fact, in many cases it is a cause of problems, but the temptation to blame the system should be avoided because it is usually the people, including the managers, and not the system that are to blame. Today, the general technology skills in an operations function are likely to be good. Most people are familiar with standard packages and should have undergone further training to be able to manage email, spreadsheets and the other packages that are most commonly used. However, the use of internal or bought-in systems is a different issue and too often inadequate training and explanation of where the technology sits in the bigger picture is provided to both operations staff and the technology teams servicing them. As a result, technology is delivering in many organisations probably only 60% or less of the benefits that it could provide.

The operations manager has a key role to play in shaping

both the technology used and how it is used. That said, there is some technology that is provided by external vendors, often with little or no ability to bespoke the system. In this case the ability to take data from these systems and use alternative capabilities to produce the required data, processes, controls and client facing documentation becomes crucially important.

In some respects the technology used within the industry can be very standard, and yet it is the ability to differentiate technology and its use that sets one firm apart from the rest. As a result there are firms with highly sophisticated internally developed systems that service both internal needs and, crucially, offer various technology-based services and products to the client base. These systems offer a clear commercial advantage but frequently at a significant cost. Technology is not cheap, so the development of technology-based client service products needs very careful analysis in order to ascertain the true costs and benefits. The provision of services like custody, prime brokerage and third-party clearing rely on the effectiveness of technology for commercial advantage and in order to be cost-effective. One reason that some firms have pulled out of custody or do not offer a prime brokerage service is the huge cost of developing and maintaining the technology infrastructure needed to support such services. Even in the general operations function the cost of upgrading technology to meet growth, market changes, client requests and regulatory require-ments can make business managers look at the option of outsourcing rather than committing to a significant expenditure.

It is not surprising therefore that the operations manager must be in a position to manage technology effectively.

In Chapter 10 (on management information) the benefits of good data and systems to receive, reformat, generate and manage such data is set out and achieving this benefit forms a key objective for the manager and the business.

Managing Technology in the Operations Function (Loader/Biggs, published by Butterworth-Heinemann) examined some of the specific and broad issues that the manager faces when it comes to technology. On data protection it states:

Elsewhere there are changes to the technology issue that are not specifically process based. Data protection is a crucial subject as contravention of the rights of individuals and corporates to confidentiality is a massive legal and business issue.

The holding or storage of data and subsequent use is governed by law. Operations teams are in possession of data related to clients both in terms of their positions and information about the client, including personal details like address as well as banking details. It is clearly obvious that managers must be (a) aware of the issues surrounding client data and (b) have devised procedures and educated staff in the primary issues related to such data.

The security over client data is partially an issue of access to the relevant areas of the database and partially about the procedures of distribution of data related to clients. As such the managers must ensure that prudent controls exist that will give adequate security but do not impact adversely on the day to day processes of the operations teams. Access risk is part of technology risk in terms of operational risk.

Technology is both power and danger. It gives advantages that can be exploited and causes problems that can be devastating. It drives operations but can equally be a constraint and it can be costly if not managed correctly.

These and other issues will be further explored later in the chapter.

Technology in operations is basically about two very different perspectives.

First, there is the operations team's use of technology for processing and MI and, second, there is the technology team's function of building and maintaining systems for use by the business. Of all the things that affect operations performance, technology is the biggest friend and at the same time can be a nightmare. Of all the things that affect technology teams the inability of operations to understand and use technology is probably the biggest issue. Yet, it is not difficult to see why both of these should be the case.

Operations understand the business of operations but usually not the technology utilised, whilst technology teams understand systems but not the business of operations. Not a happy scenario for the business!

The operations manager is charged with managing technology effectively. This includes what technology is needed and how that technology is used. It also requires the introduction of training and competency within the team so that the benefits are realised and, just as importantly, an awareness of the scope that the systems have.

Technology risk is a key element of a firm's operational risk and, therefore, a team that operates with technology it does not understand is a risk to the business. Equally, having high levels of competency and understanding of the capability of the systems requires adequate controls to be in place. This is true of the normal operation of technology, but is equally true when technology projects are taking place as they very often will be.

It is unlikely that any operations manager will not be involved in a major technology project at some stage in their career and quite likely that they will be involved in many projects of varying size and implication to the operations function. The projects may involve enhancements to existing systems or a complete change of system. There are important issues here for the manager.

How is the technology project to be effectively managed with the minimum amount of disruption to the function and with the minimum amount of risk to the business?

Planning for any project requires careful considerations above and beyond scope, timing and management and then efficient organisation of its implementation. Technology projects are no different in general terms. What are the key stages of a typical technology project?

An operations function is using technology in different ways and often makes use of different systems and/or data generated from systems for everything from trade capture to client statements. In most organisations the sheer volume of data and use of that data means that networks are used to enable the sharing and flow of critical and not so critical data to occur. As a consequence the technology structure within an organisation can look very akin to a spider's web with a core from which many strands then link. Often, particular products cannot be handled by the main system or systems used and so a separate or stand-alone system is utilised which may be as simple as a spreadsheet.

The first thing on the agenda when any technology project is being considered must be the impact that the project will have. This is clearly a double-sided question as the operations manager is first and foremost thinking about how the project will change and benefit the function and then, at the same time, considering the potential impact that the project may have on other systems and users of the data. Some but not all projects can have far-reaching consequences and particularly so in large global businesses where any major system changes or enhancements will be 'rolled out' across the organisation.

Most managers are aware of technology changes that they would like to introduce. For various reasons these changes may be difficult or impossible to bring to fruition or at least will have a long lead time to implementation.

A complete change of system may have many plus points for the operations processes and therefore efficiency and risk control, not to mention being cost-effective. However, there are reasons why the manager may need to be cautious.

Consider the project logistics.

- When will the project be started and what is the lead time to full implementation?
- What resource is needed from operations to support the project?
- What are the quality assurance parameters?
- What level of resource is needed for adequate testing?
- Will parallel running be feasible?
- Can resource be made available from operations to run both legacy and new systems for whatever period is needed?
- Will consultants and/or contractors be needed for the project?
- If so, what budget is available and where can suitable consultants be sourced?
- What will change as a result of the project being implemented?
- Who is affected, how and when?
- Is implementation planned to be staggered or is it a big-bang approach?
- What are the risk implications?
- How will retraining be managed and what will be used to gauge competency prior to implementation?
- What are the new procedures?
- How and when will they be documented?

These are just a few of the many considerations about a major, and in many cases minor, project. It is perhaps easy to see why the big issues revolve around cost, time and resource. Cost/benefit analysis may suggest that the project is justified in the long term, but the short-term costs need careful management if the budget is not to be exceeded.

Costs are always an issue, but so too is when a project should be started and how it is resourced as far as the operations area is concerned.

TIMING AND RESOURCING

There will be few businesses in the financial services industry where there will be a best time to undertake a major technology project. To some extent the timing is dictated by the commercial needs which in turn are driven by change or client pressure to provide a service. The latter can be caused by overselling by the front office or of course operations where client services teams are selling clearing, settlement and custody products. In this case the operations manager should have suitably trained the personnel concerned to understand the realities of offering and delivering technology-based services. Even so, the pressure of selling in a competitive market still leads to promises being made that can be a real challenge to deliver.

As a result, the manager must be prepared for several issues that they will need to deal with surrounding the project team and the operations team including those personnel from the operations function that will need to be permanently or periodically seconded to the project.

Problems concerning pressures on time and on the availability of operations people to a project usually result in every project. As a result, there is often some kind of slippage in the project's duration and problems are therefore bound to occur. As key people are needed more and more to keep the project on time, so the operations manager is faced with having to run the operations function underresourced and at an unacceptable risk and/or performance level or recruit temporary resource in what is bound to be seen by some as a knee jerk reaction that will cause problems rather than solve them. Neither scenario is particularly desirable nor recommended, given the importance and capital impact of increased operational risk. There is also a real danger of an adverse knock-on effect on the morale and performance of the operations team caused by a prolonged period of disruption and difficulties caused by the delays to the project. Once the buy-in of the operations team and the credibility of the project has been lost, there will be a real difficulty for the managers to contend with.

This issue needed to be considered at the planning stage when additional resource could have been introduced earlier and been ready to play a full part in the support of the day-to-day operations function as and when people were required on the project.

LOSS OF KEY PERSONNEL

Whilst on the subject of people, a loss of a key operations or project team member once the project is up and running can have massive implications. All too often, there are individuals in a project team that become the expertise and thus a major risk. What contingency will the project and or operations manager (they may be one and the same) plan? Any senior manager reviewing a project proposal will want to see that this subject has been identified and addressed. If it is not, the cost impact of delay and reworking areas of the project can be crippling.

Taking time to work cover into the project for each key person and each critical task or phase is reasonably easy to implement at the outset of the project, but significantly more difficult and expensive once the project is underway.

Many firms found this out during the Y2K projects as a shortage of people and a rapidly approaching deadline had the effect of making project managers and technicians leave one project to go to another, often at a critical point in the project cycle.

MANAGING THE OPERATIONS FUNCTION THROUGH THE PROJECT

For the operations manager and the operations function to get the best out of technology, operations needs to co-ordinate its information technology (*IT*) requirements across the whole department, so that a prioritisation of IT projects can be made. This will enable the technology department to understand the requirement and work towards delivering projects according to the priorities given by the operations department.

Importantly, it also enables both operations and technology to focus on where projects become interdependent so that project work can be properly co-ordinated.

When a firm has, as it often does, several key initiatives running simultaneously, the management of development and implementation becomes a crucial factor. A delay or problem with the development or implementation of one initiative can have a serious knock-on effect on others. As we have already noted, in a global business where the roll-out of projects and implementations has to be completed on time, serious risk and costs can be involved by poor co-ordination of initiatives by either operations or technology or both.

In the initial stages the evaluation of the project scope will have determined some of the primary roles and responsibilities of operations. Deliverables will have been agreed and, once committed to, operations must be prepared to accept that changes are not possible except in dire situations. This can be difficult given that operations work in an often rapidly changing environment and, as some projects can be of quite long duration, circumstances can and do change. Obviously, there cannot just be a blind approach that means the project trundles on irrespective of changed circumstances, but it should be appreciated that wholesale changes to technology projects can only be justified in exceptional situations.

Once such a situation becomes apparent then operations and technology must take the most effective decision for the business, even if that is writing off a large chunk of the development budget. This is better than completing a project that cannot and does not deliver what is needed.

The operations manager has considerable responsibilities then, and these include making sure that the key team members have sufficient business skills to appreciate how the project must be evolved. Seeking or obtaining the views of a key system user may seem an obvious requirement, but so often these views are held by middle or junior staff. A poor manager will fail to get this vital input at all or, more likely, it will arise long after the project is underway. All credibility is gone both within the operations team and also within the technology team who discover they have wasted hours of work.

The bottom line is that really extensive research, evaluation and discussion with a broad representative element of the operations team must form the base of the preparatory stage of any technology project.

From that point on there needs to be a constant monitoring of progress and dissemination of the progress to all team members. The pressure on people to continue with their current tasks, retrain for the revised tasks and deal with any parallel running is not to be underestimated. The manager has to lead the project in every sense and this will include making sure everyone receives relevant information about the project status.

This is important because while client service teams need to keep clients aware of the developments, risk managers will be monitoring the increased risk levels throughout the project and team leaders will be scheduling the retraining programs.

As the project reaches an advanced stage the emphasis will change to managing the implementation. There will be a roll-out program for the project, be it an upgrade or a major replacement, and by now the operations manager should have the team fully briefed and ready to undertake the testing and parallel running.

A crucial factor in any technology project will be the sign-off of various phases of the project. The manager will oversee this task in conjunction with the supervisors and other team members designated at the planning stage.

Box 7.1 shows the project flow:

Box 7.1 Project flow.	
1 Scope	7 User acceptance testing
2 Requirements definition	8 Performance testing
3 Design and build	9 Regression testing
4 Unit testing	10 Conversion
5 System testing	11 Implementation
6 Integration testing	

Source: *Managing Technology in the Operations Function* (Butterworth-Heinemann).

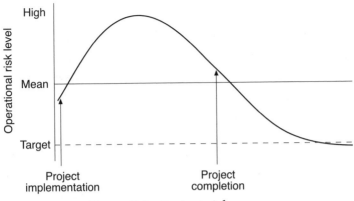

Figure 7.1 Project risk wave.
Source: the**dsc**.portfolio.

POST-IMPLEMENTATION

The post-implementation period is as important as the rest of the project. Risk and performance levels in the operations change during this period as the risk wave in Figure 7.1 shows. The operations manager is seeking to bend the wave down and then below the risk threshold within the target time set.

TECHNOLOGY AND THE FUTURE

Technology developments are shaping the operations function of tomorrow. The impact of technology has dramatically changed many markets, replacing the traditional open-outcry trading with electronic dealing systems that allow not only cheaper trading by removing the cost of floor teams but also by allowing access from locations outside the country where the market is domiciled. Massive volumes on some markets such as the derivatives exchanges have resulted because of the greater capacity afforded by dealing systems. This change is mirrored in the operations function through the concepts of straight-through-processing, remote clearing and paperless settlement. Another major driver has been the need to produce and distribute information.

In other chapters in this book the importance of management information to enable effective risk management, planning, client service and business development has been raised. This business driver continues and, therefore, so does the need for technology to produce solutions that:

- reduce costs;
- increase capacity;
- meet market and clearing developments;
- manage risk;
- enhance client services;
- support global business;
- maintain the market leader status of the firm.

A significant number of the technology projects that will support the above will be operations-based, particularly as the market and clearing infrastructures change and securities and derivatives become consolidated, leading in turn to the need for multi-product settlement systems in a unified operations environment.

Only the managers that embrace technology and have the vision to develop it will be prepared for the changes and challenges that operations face in the coming years. Technology drives businesses, operations managers drive technology. Making it happen is the challenge.

Chapter

8

· ·

PROCEDURAL DOCUMENTATION – CAPTURING THE KNOWLEDGE BASE

An organisation's knowledge base is its most valuable asset.

Laurie Saxey, the**dsc**.portfolio

This chapter examines the need for good procedural documentation, its benefits, defining characteristics of good documentation and issues that the manager will need to address when embarking upon a documentation project.

In short, we will consider how good documentation can assist in capturing that most valuable and elusive of the firm's assets: the knowledge residing in its skilled employees and in its corporate culture.

THE HISTORICAL PERSPECTIVE

Although there would now be few managers within our industry who would deny that effective procedural documentation is, in principle, a good thing, this has not always been the case.

Before Big Bang, many securities trading firms were small partnerships with few employees. The typical firm of this type traded only in UK equities with the luxury of a 2-week settlement cycle. There was little oversight of the firm's activities imposed either by regulators or by the internal audit function (if indeed one existed) and perceptions of the risks inherent in trading and settlement activities were only just starting to be fully understood.

Documentation was often produced in an *ad hoc* manner by operational staff in response to an immediate fire-fighting need and was discarded when the immediate crisis had passed. A typical example of this approach is the back-of-the-envelope bullet point list produced to cover a holiday absence.

Even in those firms that recognised some need for procedural documentation, typically it was a low-priority issue and had little claim on the firm's budget. There was no consistency of style or structure across documentation produced in different functional areas within the organisation and there was no central repository of any documentation that had been produced.

Notwithstanding the advent of more demanding regulation, more complex instruments and a generally more professional approach to the requirements of best practice and good management, it is still regrettably possible to find outposts of these attitudes in some of the otherwise highly professional organisations in the industry.

THE BENEFITS OF GOOD DOCUMENTATION

There are a number of benefits that are associated with maintaining good procedural documentation.

- *The knowledge base.* As noted above, every successful firm has invested substantial resources in recruiting highly qualified staff and has developed its own unique approach to delivering a high quality of service to its clients. Effective procedural documentation enables the firm to capture that expertise and make it readily accessible across the organisation.

- *Compliance with regulatory requirements and best practice.* There are few aspects of the industry that are not regulated in some way and even those activities that are not directly regulated must conform to the firm's standards of efficiency and security. Good procedural documentation enables compliance officers to ensure that activities comply with regulatory requirements and managers to ensure that the firm's internal standards are being observed. Once best practice has been codified, there can be no doubts as to the appropriate procedures to be used in carrying out an activity and the procedure may be infinitely reproduced to the same standard.

- *Identifying and controlling areas of risk.* Systematic control weaknesses or less serious departures from best practice, that may otherwise have not been explicit, become readily apparent during the process of documenting an activity. Good documentation provides a convenient source of information for those concerned with assessing and controlling operational weaknesses.

- *Re-engineering.* Whenever process re-engineering is undertaken, the existence of high-quality documentation of the firm's activities can substantially reduce the analysis phase of the project. Indeed, it may have been inefficiencies that were identified by the documentation process that generated the requirement to undertake the re-engineering process.

- *Audit process.* Auditors, both internal and external, are able to use an organisation's procedural documentation (if of sufficiently good quality) to reduce the time required to audit an activity or functional area. Any control weaknesses or recommendations for improvement that are identified during the audit can be cross-referenced to the relevant documented procedure. As a result, the required procedural changes can be speedily made and immediately reflected in the procedure manual.

- *Senior management's professional responsibilities.* The increasing complexity of the financial services industry requires that the senior manager (who may necessarily be somewhat removed from the day-to-day processing activities of the organisation) has access to a reliable source of information about the areas for which they are responsible. Good procedural documentation provides this reference source.

- *Line manager's responsibilities.* Good procedural documentation aids a line manager in fully understanding and complying with the obligations and responsibilities of their role.

- *Training.* Procedural documentation is an ideal resource for training new, temporary or established staff, thus reducing the training time necessary to reach the required skill standard.

- *Recruitment.* The skill set required to carry out documented activities is readily apparent from good procedural documentation and can be used as an aid to the production of job descriptions or candidate selection.

- *Business continuity.* Procedural documentation can form a valuable input into the firm's disaster recovery plan.

WHAT IS GOOD PROCEDURAL DOCUMENTATION?

- *Good procedural documentation satisfies the needs of its audience.* Before embarking on any documentation project, you should consider carefully who the intended audience is and to what purpose the documents will be put. For example, operations staff will typically turn to documentation to establish how to carry out a task with which they are unfamiliar in the absence of a colleague. If the document does not clearly identify all of the steps required to complete the task, it will clearly not have satisfied its audience. If the target audience is senior management, there is likely to be a lesser requirement for such detail.

    Although the majority of procedural documentation is produced in text format, some thought should be given to the use of flow diagrams in place of or in addition to text. The way in which the flow diagram is constructed should take account of the expected level of familiarity with such diagrams on the part of the intended audience.

- *Good procedural documentation is integrated into the culture of the organisation.* No matter how good procedural documentation is, it has little use if potential users do not recognise its value. Integrating procedural documentation into the structure of an organisation means encouraging ownership; thus, a mechanism should exist for users to report changes and suggest improvements. The existence of the documentation should be well publicised within the organisation and potential users should be encouraged to make use of it and integrate it into their daily activities.

- *Good procedural documentation is well-structured.* It is a defining feature of good procedural documentation that it is logically structured and written in a style that is clear and accessible to its intended audience. Poorly structured procedures are likely to generate errors and misunderstandings. In addition, a common style and structure should be applied across the organisation so that users become familiar with it.

- *Good procedural documentation is well-maintained and controlled.* Failure to put in place a mechanism for regularly updating the procedures manual will eventually lead to out-of-date documentation that will be of little use to the audience and will be potentially misleading.

  It is similarly important to give some thought to a method of controlling the documentation once it has been put in place to ensure that different versions are not in issue simultaneously. These concerns are addressed in greater detail later in this chapter – see 'Maintaining, controlling and distributing the documentation' (p. 152).

IN-HOUSE OR OUTSOURCE?

In an industry increasingly concerned with cost/benefit analysis and governed by budgetary constraints, there will inevitably come a point when the manager must decide whether to produce the required procedural documentation in-house – for example, by making use of departmental managers – or to employ an external specialist firm.

Each of these approaches has its own benefits and disadvantages – and it is these concerns that we will look at now. We shall compare the typical in-house strategy of using departmental managers/supervisors to produce the procedural documentation as against using a specialist documentation consultancy.

There are three key considerations that the decision maker must take into account when deciding which route would fit their circumstance.

1   Skill

Whilst it will not be difficult to identify managers/supervisors with the required practical skills associated with their areas of responsibility, it may not be so easy to identify those to whom authoring skills come naturally. You should assess carefully the proposed author's ability to produce clear, concise, user-friendly documentation to a pre-defined standard and format that is consistent across functional areas.

Notwithstanding a degree of presumption of skill on the part of an external consultancy, you should discuss the consultancy's previous documentation projects and possibly ask for generic examples of the standard of documentation produced. A good-quality consultancy will have a defined and well-validated methodology for the collection of data.

It is similarly important to arrange for regular quality reviews of the consultancy's output so that you can be sure that it meets your requirements.

2 Time

In common with most requirements within the industry, whenever a need is identified the delivery time is typically immediately.

Firms in today's securities industry typically run their businesses with very little spare staff capacity, if any. The line manager/supervisor and their staff may therefore have little time to devote to such issues as producing a procedure manual. If a decision is taken to produce documentation using line managers, consideration should be given to releasing the authors from their normal duties until the documentation project is at least well advanced. At the very least clear delivery deadlines should be set and progress periodically reviewed.

Whilst a dedicated external consultancy will be able to provide full-time resources to the documentation project, it is important to agree deadlines upfront and to put in place an agreed progress reporting mechanism.

3 Cost

The overriding criterion here must of course be value for money. This is perhaps the most difficult of the criteria to quantify and care must be taken carefully to assess the relative benefits of the two approaches and the likelihood of achieving the desired outcome.

The cost of in-house staff time will be well-known and no special budget allocation need be sought. However, the opportunity cost of diverting staff resources away from their core activities should also be taken into account, as should the amount of time taken to produce a product of a quality comparable with an external specialist consultancy.

The costs of using an external specialist will be easily established and will represent an 'all-in' cost. It is likely, however, that a request for a budget allocation to complete the project will have to be made in competition with the many other demands on the corporate pocket.

MAINTAINING, CONTROLLING AND DISTRIBUTING THE DOCUMENTATION

Out-of-date and unmaintained procedural documentation not only represents a waste of the original resource devoted to producing it, but also is likely to be the cause of possibly costly error. To be of ongoing value, your procedures must be reviewed regularly and the supporting documentation updated to reflect changes in practice or policy. This may be achieved by associating a next review due date with each procedure. The period between reviews is to some extent subjective, but best practice would indicate a maximum period between reviews of no more than 1 year. If a major change occurs in the interim – e.g., structural reorganisation or the introduction of a new IT system – review of the affected procedures should take place immediately.

Whilst it is important to encourage local ownership by the users, the situation where there are a number of different versions of a procedure existing simultaneously around the organisation must be avoided. There are a number of methods of achieving this, but perhaps the simplest is to have a central online repository of procedures that acts as the definitive reference source. This repository should be under centralised control, and the numbers of those able to amend a procedure must be strictly limited. Additionally, each version should be clearly identified by a unique version number or date, so that users can be in no doubt as to the most recent version. Some attention must also be given to the means by which the procedural documentation will be distributed. Paper-based documentation is an option, but if the users have access to a centralised depositary via a corporate intranet, access to the most recent issue will be facilitated. In addition, a number of commercially available document management applications are available that can run either stand-alone or across an intranet. Such applications typically have mechanisms for controlling update access to the documents, for notifying users of a new version and for archiving reference copies of superseded versions.

Chapter

9

....

CLIENT MANAGEMENT

Developing and managing a successful client facing product is an art not an exact science; years of building the successful product will involve teams of people and yet it can be undone by a moment of indiscipline or madness by a single person.

David Loader

Managing the client facing side of any business is not particularly easy. There are many potential problems that can and will occur. Some of these may not be directly under the control of or have been created by the firm that has the relationship with the client.

It is important to understand the relationship from both angles – i.e., between client and counterparty, and counterparty and client. This is simply because the relationship looks different depending from where you are viewing it. Many operations teams have client facing roles and, even if the client relationships are managed by a separate team, the interaction between operations and the client facing team is crucial. Operations teams themselves are of course frequently clients. This is certainly the case with custodians, technology providers and banks.

Operations managers need to consider operational risk when they are thinking about the client relationships they deal with. Reputations are made over time and lost in seconds. Providing inferior services in a competitive environment is a recipe for disaster, and that disaster can manifest itself over time, so that if the manager and the team are not monitoring and managing relationships they will be unaware of the problem until it is too late.

There can also be a tendency for operations personnel to view internal clients differently from external clients. This is highly dangerous and creates a split client culture that assumes inferior service to internal clients is not important. Nothing could be further from the truth and the operations manager must ensure that this kind of complacency is eradicated before it becomes a major issue in the firm. To reinforce the point, the operations manager can simply point out that outsourcing is a very real option for many firms.

Good operations managers understand the importance of client relationships – both inward and outward relationships – and can develop good practice by the teams directly and indirectly involved. This is important as the big picture needs to be understood by everyone. A client is a client of the firm, usually utilising more than one product of the firm. The ability of the firm to draw together its products and services and deliver a uniform quality of service to the client is crucial to the overall success of the firm in gaining and retaining business. Operations teams contribute to this process, and they must be aware of the role and the roles of others in providing the overall product.

Understanding what client relationships are is the first step to achieving this awareness.

CUSTOMER RELATIONSHIPS

What are the key issues in a client relationship?

The answer is, of course: many, if not all, issues are key to one or other party and sometimes to both parties. It is easy to assume that cost and accuracy are paramount, and this is certainly the case with accuracy, but not always true when looking at cost. Cost is relevant, but the quality of the service is also crucial. Other issues are important too.

The key issues in respect of customer relationships include:

- the approach to client service and establishing a customer-orientated culture;
- the understanding of the client's organisational and business structure;
- the risk impact of providing added value client services;
- measuring client risk;
- introducing controls and procedures to ensure performance standards;
- providing a competitive edge to the business;
- dealing with complaints.

These issues are of great importance. As we have already noted, the ability of a business to retain and gain clients relies heavily on all aspects of customer relationship. The service provided out of the operations area will be judged by the client as part of the overall service provided by the organisation; in other words, reputation is made or lost by what operations do or don't do.

The operations manager needs to recognise that managing and supervising customer relationships successfully revolves around:

- choice of personnel;
- definition of the client service function;

- structure of the client service team or group;
- adequate training in key relationship skills;
- understanding of the client's business;
- policy and procedures for identifying and dealing with problems;
- relationship management policy.

Without the above it will be impossible for the manager/ supervisor to monitor the service levels provided against the client requirements. As a result, relationship management will be more difficult than it should be and there will be a real chance that the relationship may deteriorate and, ultimately, the client will move away. Providing a high-quality client service is usually a full-time role for a dedicated team of people. It is not therefore something that can be provided without a clearly defined policy and an adequate budget. More importantly, the interaction between this dedicated team and the other areas of operations that support its role is absolutely crucial.

The manager needs to be very careful in managing people. The client facing team should be highly focused on client service. Individuals in other areas may not have the same level of focus because they do not deal directly with the clients. When something goes wrong it is easy for the issue to escalate into a finger pointing exercise between different areas of operations or between operations and other parts of the firm. Obviously, this is undesirable and indicates a fault in the management style, as clearly the importance of teamwork and mutual understanding of responsibilities and roles in delivering client service have not been understood by the individuals concerned.

The client has no time for internal problems and will not expect to suffer from such issues. They also expect to see a company service rather than individual services. The products – like prime brokerage – make much of the one-stop shop concept which is a powerful marketing point. If the service then disintegrates because the firm's individual areas operate without any concept of collective roles and responsibilities the client will move away and the reputation of the product will suffer.

The customer relationship policy of the organisation therefore must encompass both front office and operations, so that the client is aware only of the company service. High degrees of personal and business skills are therefore required in the operations team, in general, and the client facing team, in particular. Training individuals, supervisors and managers so that they will develop an understanding of the complex and crucial role of relationship management is vitally important. Developing a suitable and practical approach to client relationships and the client culture itself are also vital.

THE APPROACH TO CUSTOMER RELATIONSHIPS AND THE 'CLIENT CULTURE'

It helps if we first seek to define what we mean by a 'client culture' (Box 9.1).

> *Box 9.1* Definition of 'client culture'.
>
> A culture within and across an organisation that places the relationship with a client as the key to growth and profitability of the organisation, and one which is totally supported, resourced, implemented and managed by senior personnel in all areas of the business.
>
> *Source*: the**dsc**.portfolio.

If we look at the industry approach to customer relationships and the establishing of a client culture, we will see that in general terms they are driven by market considerations as well as corporate policy. High on the agenda of business managers is the need for either market share or adequate generation of prime revenue from the client base. Both have fundamentally different implications for the way in which the client facing policy will be formulated.

We must also consider that added to this equation are the market-driven and what we might call 'dictated' customer service issues. This leads into analysing whether or not a particular business sector or type of client service is intrinsically profit-driven or accepted as part of a wider profit generation capability on the back of proprietary trading.

Operations managers can find that, today, operational areas are just as much likely to be structured as revenue generators as they are service/administration providers. At one end of the scale there are organisations that have operations-based client teams contributing significant revenue to the business by selling services and products independently from the sales teams. At the other end, client teams operating in traditional structures are providing the support and service levels that contribute to the company's core product.

One might think there would be a significant variance to the approach to the relationships from two very different set-ups, and yet in reality there will be little if any difference. Customer business is won or lost for many reasons. A company failing to provide the client with the service they want and expect, or being unable to recognise and encompass change that requires new services and products will lose that client, whether or not they are revenue- or cost-based as a team. It is the service not the structure that is important and service depends on the culture possessed by the team. The comforting factor is that most managers and supervisors consider themselves customer-orientated. This is because their function is to head up a team that serves others. However, we have already alluded to the fact that what we think and what the customer thinks are potentially two very different viewpoints. Understanding the client, its business, its structure, its people and its objectives is vitally important. So, too, is perception.

To that end we have to recognise that the client needs to believe that the service being provided is:

- as much for their benefit as the supplier;
- is supported by personnel that understand the client's profile;
- is able to offer innovative solutions to problems;

- can be expanded and adapted to meet the growth in the client's business;
- is 'tailored' for the client.

Whether the client is in-house or external, the above are all true. It cannot be stressed enough that the manager must make sure there is no differentiation in approach to internal and external clients. There is often a misconception about the importance of treating in-house relationships on the same basis as external client relationships.

In many cases the principal activity is not only significant but also dependent on an efficient post-transaction process to prevent unnecessary additional costs that will impact on profitability. There should be a clear policy that house clients receive a service in exactly the same way as an external client would expect to do so. As previously stated, it is not acceptable to treat the in-house client as tame and therefore provide a substandard service. Once again, if there is any reluctance to accept this viewpoint it may be worth reminding people that outsourcing is a very real option in today's markets.

Returning to the issue of client culture, this needs to be established by:

- setting a business objective for the organisation as a whole;
- creating teams staffed by individuals that fully understand the concepts of and are totally focused on client service;
- establishing a policy that encourages management by an innovative and industry-aware group;

- ensuring the teams are led by key managers interacting across the company.

Client satisfaction and support can be lost in a matter of months even when the relationship has been in existence for many years. The successful ongoing managing of the relationship and service is therefore crucial.

KNOW YOUR CLIENT

A key element of any client relationship is the know your client (*KYC*) factor.

Obviously, this is important in terms of developing the relationship and service, but equally important is the joint issues of money laundering and fraud.

Knowing exactly who the client is and carrying out due diligence is vitally important. The Bank for International Settlement's (*BIS*) Basel Committee published *Customer Due Diligence for Banks* in February 2003 and the reader should visit the BIS website to access this document. An attachment was published in 2005 and is reproduced here so that a good understanding of the impact of due diligence in KYC can be obtained.

General guide to account opening and customer identification

Attachment to Basel Committee Publication No. 85 *Customer Due Diligence for Banks* (February 2003):

1. The Basel Committee on Banking Supervision in its paper on *Customer Due Diligence for Banks* published in October 2001 referred to the intention of the Working Group on Cross-border Banking[1] to develop guidance on customer identification. Customer identification is an essential element of an effective customer due diligence programme which banks need to put in place to guard against reputational, operational, legal and concentration risks. It is also necessary in order to comply with anti-money laundering legal requirements and a prerequisite for the identification of bank accounts related to terrorism.

2. What follows is account opening and customer identification guidelines and a general guide to good practice based on the principles of the Basel Committee's *Customer Due Diligence for Banks* paper. This document, which has been developed by the Working Group on Cross-border Banking, does not cover every eventuality, but instead focuses on some of the mechanisms that banks can use in developing an effective customer identification programme.

3. These guidelines represent a starting point for supervisors and banks in the area of customer identification. This document does not address the

---

[1] The Working Group on Cross-border Banking is a joint group consisting of members of the Basel Committee and of the Offshore Group of Banking Supervisors. *Source*: BIS. A copy of the Committee's *Consolidated KYC Risk Management* publication can be found in Appendix C.

other elements of the *Customer Due Diligence for Banks* paper, such as the ongoing monitoring of accounts. However, these elements should be considered in the development of effective customer due diligence, anti-money laundering and combating the financing of terrorism procedures.

4. These guidelines may be adapted for use by national supervisors who are seeking to develop or enhance customer identification programmes. However, supervisors should recognise that any customer identification programme should reflect the different types of customers (individual vs. institution) and the different levels of risk resulting from a customer's relationship with a bank. Higher risk transactions and relationships, such as those with politically exposed persons or organisations, will clearly require greater scrutiny than lower risk transactions and accounts.

5. Guidelines and best practices created by national supervisors should also reflect the various types of transactions that are most prevalent in the national banking system. For example, non-face-to-face opening of accounts may be more prevalent in one country than another. For this reason the customer identification procedures may differ between countries.

6. Some identification documents are more vulnerable to fraud than others. For those that are most susceptible to fraud, or where there is

uncertainty concerning the validity of the document(s) presented, the bank should verify the information provided by the customer through additional inquiries or other sources of information.

7. Customer identification documents should be retained for at least 5 years after an account is closed. All financial transaction records should be retained for at least 5 years after the transaction has taken place.

8. These guidelines are divided into two sections covering different aspects of customer identification. Section A describes what types of information should be collected and verified for natural persons seeking to open accounts or perform transactions. Section B describes what types of information should be collected and verified for institutions, and is in two parts – the first relating to corporate vehicles and the second to other types of institutions.

9. All the terms used in these guidelines have the same meaning as in the *Customer Due Diligence for Banks* paper.

A. Natural persons

10. For natural persons the following information should be obtained, where applicable:

    o legal name and any other names used (such as maiden name);

- correct permanent address (the full address should be obtained; a Post Office box number is not sufficient);
- telephone number, fax number and email address;
- date and place of birth;
- nationality;
- occupation, public position held and/or name of employer;
- an official personal identification number or other unique identifier contained in an unexpired official document (e.g., passport, identification card, residence permit, social security records, driving licence) that bears a photograph of the customer;
- type of account and nature of the banking relationship;
- signature.

11. The bank should verify this information by at least one of the following methods:

- confirming the date of birth from an official document (e.g., birth certificate, passport, identity card, social security records);
- confirming the permanent address (e.g., utility bill, tax assessment, bank statement, a letter from a public authority);
- contacting the customer by telephone, by letter or by email to confirm the information supplied after an account has been opened (e.g., a disconnected phone, returned mail or incorrect

email address should warrant further investigation);

- o confirming the validity of the official documentation provided through certification by an authorised person (e.g., embassy official, notary public).

12. The examples quoted above are not the only possibilities. In particular jurisdictions there may be other documents of an equivalent nature which may be produced as satisfactory evidence of customers' identity.

13. Financial institutions should apply equally effective customer identification procedures for non-face-to-face customers as for those available for interview.

14. From the information provided in paragraph 10, financial institutions should be able to make an initial assessment of a customer's risk profile. Particular attention needs to be focused on those customers identified thereby as having a higher risk profile and additional inquiries made or information obtained in respect of those customers to include the following:

- o evidence of an individual's permanent address sought through a credit reference agency search, or through independent verification by home visits;
- o personal reference (i.e., by an existing customer of the same institution);

- ○ prior bank reference and contact with the bank regarding the customer;
- ○ source of wealth;
- ○ verification of employment, public position held (where appropriate).

15. For one-off or occasional transactions where the amount of the transaction or series of linked transactions does not exceed an established minimum monetary value, it might be sufficient to require and record only name and address.

16. It is important that the customer acceptance policy is not so restrictive that it results in a denial of access by the general public to banking services, especially for people who are financially or socially disadvantaged.

B. Institutions

17. The underlying principles of customer identification for natural persons have equal application to customer identification for all institutions. Where in the following the identification and verification of natural persons is involved, the foregoing guidance in respect of such persons should have equal application.

18. The term institution includes any entity that is not a natural person. In considering the customer identification guidance for the different types of institutions, particular attention should be given to the different levels of risk involved.

I. Corporate entities

19. For corporate entities (i.e., corporations and partnerships), the following information should be obtained:

    o name of institution;
    o principal place of institution's business operations;
    o mailing address of institution;
    o contact telephone and fax numbers;
    o some form of official identification number, if available (e.g., tax identification number);
    o the original or certified copy of the Certificate of Incorporation and Memorandum and Articles of Association;
    o the resolution of the Board of Directors to open an account and identification of those who have authority to operate the account;
    o nature and purpose of business and its legitimacy.

20. The bank should verify this information by at least one of the following methods:

    o for established corporate entities – reviewing a copy of the latest report and accounts (audited, if available);
    o conducting an enquiry by a business information service, or an undertaking from a reputable and known firm of lawyers or accountants confirming the documents submitted;

- undertaking a company search and/or other commercial enquiries to see that the institution has not been, or is not in the process of being, dissolved, struck off, wound up or terminated;
- utilising an independent information verification process, such as by accessing public and private databases;
- obtaining prior bank references;
- visiting the corporate entity, where practical;
- contacting the corporate entity by telephone, mail or email.

21. The bank should also take reasonable steps to verify the identity and reputation of any agent that opens an account on behalf of a corporate customer, if that agent is not an officer of the corporate customer.

Corporations/Partnerships

22. For corporations/partnerships, the principal guidance is to look behind the institution to identify those who have control over the business and the company's/partnership's assets, including those who have ultimate control. For corporations, particular attention should be paid to shareholders, signatories, or others who inject a significant proportion of the capital or financial support or otherwise exercise control. Where the owner is another corporate entity or trust, the objective is to undertake reasonable measures to look behind that company or entity and to verify the identity

of the principals. What constitutes control for this purpose will depend on the nature of a company, and may rest in those who are mandated to manage funds, accounts or investments without requiring further authorisation, and who would be in a position to override internal procedures and control mechanisms. For partnerships, each partner should be identified and it is also important to identify immediate family members that have ownership control.

23. Where a company is listed on a recognised stock exchange or is a subsidiary of such a company then the company itself may be considered to be the principal to be identified. However, consideration should be given to whether there is effective control of a listed company by an individual, small group of individuals or another corporate entity or trust. If this is the case then those controllers should also be considered to be principals and identified accordingly.

II. Other types of institution

24. For the account categories referred to in paragraphs 26 to 34, the following information should be obtained in addition to that required to verify the identity of the principals:

   o name of account;
   o mailing address;

- contact telephone and fax numbers;
- some form of official identification number, if available (e.g., tax identification number);
- description of the purpose/activities of the account holder (e.g., in a formal constitution);
- copy of documentation confirming the legal existence of the account holder (e.g., register of charities).

25. The bank should verify this information by at least one of the following:

- obtaining an independent undertaking from a reputable and known firm of lawyers or accountants confirming the documents submitted;
- obtaining prior bank references;
- accessing public and private databases or official sources.

Retirement benefit programmes

26. Where an occupational pension programme, employee benefit trust or share option plan is an applicant for an account the trustee and any other person who has control over the relationship (e.g., administrator, programme manager and account signatories) should be considered as principals and the bank should take steps to verify their identities.

Mutuals/Friendly societies, co-operatives and provident societies

27. Where these entities are an applicant for an account, the principals to be identified should be considered to be those persons exercising control or significant influence over the organisation's assets. This will often include board members plus executives and account signatories.

Charities, clubs and associations

28. In the case of accounts to be opened for charities, clubs and societies, the bank should take reasonable steps to identify and verify at least two signatories along with the institution itself. The principals who should be identified should be considered to be those persons exercising control or significant influence over the organisation's assets. This will often include members of a governing body or committee, the president, any board members, the treasurer and all signatories.

29. In all cases independent verification should be obtained that the persons involved are true representatives of the institution. Independent confirmation should also be obtained of the purpose of the institution.

Trusts and foundations

30. When opening an account for a trust, the bank
    should take reasonable steps to verify the
    trustee(s), the settlor(s) of the trust (including any
    persons settling assets into the trust), any
    protector(s), beneficiary(ies) and signatories.
    Beneficiaries should be identified when they are
    defined. In the case of a foundation, steps should
    be taken to verify the founder, the managers/
    directors and the beneficiaries.

Professional intermediaries

31. When a professional intermediary opens a client
    account on behalf of a single client that client
    must be identified. Professional intermediaries
    will often open 'pooled' accounts on behalf of a
    number of entities. Where funds held by the
    intermediary are not co-mingled but where there
    are 'sub-accounts' which can be attributable to
    each beneficial owner, all beneficial owners of the
    account held by the intermediary should be
    identified. Where the funds are co-mingled, the
    bank should look through to the beneficial
    owners; however, there may be circumstances
    which should be set out in supervisory guidance
    where the bank may not need to look beyond the
    intermediary (e.g., when the intermediary is
    subject to the same due diligence standards in
    respect of its client base as the bank).

32. Where such circumstances apply and an account is opened for an open or closed ended investment company, unit trust or limited partnership which is also subject to the same due diligence standards in respect of its client base as the bank, the following should be considered as principals and the bank should take steps to identify:

   o the fund itself;
   o its directors or any controlling board where it is a company;
   o its trustee where it is a unit trust;
   o its managing (general) partner where it is a limited partnership;
   o account signatories;
   o any other person who has control over the relationship – e.g., fund administrator or manager.

33. Where other investment vehicles are involved, the same steps should be taken as in paragraph 32 where it is appropriate to do so. In addition all reasonable steps should be taken to verify the identity of the beneficial owners of the funds and of those who have control of the funds.

34. Intermediaries should be treated as individual customers of the bank and the standing of the intermediary should be separately verified by obtaining the appropriate information drawn from the itemised lists included in paragraphs 19 and 20 above.

MONEY LAUNDERING

Operations managers will of course be familiar with the anti-money laundering (*AML*) requirements through the internal AML training.

It is important, however, that the managers remain well briefed on the latest AML issues as well as refreshing their memory of the main drivers, etc., behind the AML legislation and guidance.

The Financial Action Task Force (*FATF*) has produced recommendations related to both money laundering (*ML*) and terrorist financing, extracts of which are in the appendices and should be studied. Interpretive notes are to be found on the FATF website and should also be studied.

DEFINING THE SERVICE AND ESTABLISHING RELATIONSHIPS

What is considered as client service?

One approach is to develop a service that can be a uniform product based on the basic settlement function that is tweaked to suit different types of client. This is reasonable as there are certain standard or core processes that will take place and there are common added value products like third-party clearing that can be provided.

System-supported services are important to many clients, but not so important to smaller clients as, for example, help and advice on new products, valuations and even regulatory issues. This is where the bespoking of the service enables a product to be offered to the client based on at least some of their requirements.

So, the definition of client service could be said to be:

A standard settlement relationship that is enhanced by the provision of additional services that benefit the client.

Source: the**dsc**.portfolio

We have repeatedly said that managing the relationship and service is crucial, but what is involved in the relationship?

ESTABLISHING RELATIONSHIPS

Relationships in any walk of life revolve around two key factors, trust and compatibility.

There is no change to this when we look at the relationship between a bank or broker and their clients. The fundamental issues are a belief that the relationship is mutually beneficial, is wanted and will be viewed as a long-term one.

The latter point is very important. Today, with so many system-related issues and straight-through-processing high on the agenda, clients are seeking a counterpart that they will have a significant dependency on in terms of these system-related services. It may therefore be tempting for a broker to believe that the client is locked in by the provision of technology-related services.

This may be true with some firms and clients, but it would be a mistake to assume it works every time. Clients will move if the relationship sours, whatever the cost in terms of finance and disruption. Why? Because the relationship the client has with their broker or bank or custodian is part of operational risk. Operational risk is a major concern and any substandard service or problem with a counterpart relationship cannot be tolerated by any reasonable risk management policy.

The need to establish a monitoring process of the relationship for signs of problems is therefore a key element of managing the relationship. Look at the following example (Box 9.2) and consider if this scenario could happen in your firm.

THE MANAGER'S ROLE IN RELATIONSHIP MANAGEMENT

The key issue is to develop the relationship in terms of both the team concept and the corporate concept. Clearly, the day-to-day activities will be part of the relationship, and it is here that the client culture examined earlier will be crucial. The minor issues and problems that may occur are dealt with by the contacts in both parties' operations. The way in which the operations area is structured will determine who is dealing with the client on the daily and ongoing basis.

Box 9.2 Example.

A client is experiencing a situation with the data provided by their broker that is causing them a problem in their operations function. This problem is occurring only occasionally and yet, from the broker's viewpoint, it is having an unseen, dramatic and damaging effect because the client has mentioned it, but nothing has been done to resolve the problem.

The client is being inconvenienced and is losing confidence in their broker/bank as the counterpart. The situation is not being addressed and appears, to the client anyway, as being treated as unimportant by the broker.

The client is reluctant to keep raising the matter and so, as the problem persists, they decide to gradually move their business elsewhere.

The broker may never be aware that it is the operations teams performance that was to blame.

Without adequate monitoring of performance and the relationship, there is undoubtedly a strong probability that clients will be lost when the problem could and should have been avoided.

We can look at some of the main issues that the manager needs to consider in relation to establishing an effective client relationship management function:

- The structure of the operations team.
- Who has responsibility for day-to-day client contact?
- How is the performance monitored?
- What are the escalation procedures for problems?
- Establishment of a client liaison programme.
- Interaction and co-operation with the front-office client team.
- Interaction with other areas of the firm.

- Identifying industry issues affecting or likely to affect the client.
- Training the client facing and support teams in product and service awareness.
- Analysing the competition.
- Constantly reviewing, developing and refining the client service product.

Each of these issues is very much interlinked and forms the core subjects for customer relationship building and maintenance. They will be examined in more detail.

STRUCTURE OF THE OPERATIONS FUNCTION

All operations teams will be structured differently and, yet, they will largely be performing the same functions. The client facing team may be an actual team of people dedicated to the provision of client service. Equally, it could be part of a middle-office concept or designated people within a general settlements/clearing team. The important thing is that the manager has the best structure for providing the service.

RESPONSIBILITY

In most cases a client is looking for designated contacts at different levels. Daily contact is likely to be provided by a client team with a designated representative or account manager at the next level. Overseeing the whole client

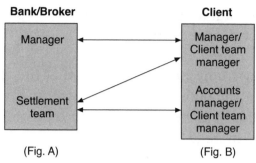

Figure 9.1 Communication lines.

team may be a supervisor and team manager reporting to the operations manager.

Figure 9.1 illustrates the clear communication lines between the client (Fig. A) and the broker (Fig. B).

It is important that the day-to-day communication is separated from senior management contact so that the people doing the processes deal with the majority of issues and problems. This is important because there can be a temptation, in the marketing of the services, for the more senior staff to offer to be the contact – which appears to be fair enough as it seems to emphasise that the client is viewed as important. Clearly, this can be flattering for the client but is almost certainly going to be the beginning of a nightmare situation whereby every issue, however minor, is automatically routed to the manager or account manager, and not the people best placed to initially review and resolve the matter. We can see therefore there is a need for the responsibilities of each team member to be defined and for the contacts and their responsibilities to be explained to the client.

This is important for external relationships but applies as well to the internal client.

Another important consideration is that the client must not feel that the door is closed to them at any level, but equally there has to be a logical order to the relationship. This may be included as part of a service level agreement if used.

Establishing the roles and responsibilities of the personnel on both sides of the relationship is fundamental to a workable and successful arrangement.

MEASURING SERVICE LEVELS

The combination of basic settlement processes and added value services makes measuring performance a complex exercise in most firms. We will cover the importance of good management information in Chapter 10 and, as far as the basic settlement processes are concerned, performance is being monitored through, for instance, workflow analysis. Benchmarking will provide the information that will highlight any potential problems the client might have experienced as a result of general performance problems.

As was seen in the earlier example (Box 9.2), the unknown is what the client has perceived as a problem or what has occurred but, for whatever reason, it is not identified in the monitoring/benchmarking. It is important to understand the client's business. Only by doing this will the client facing team be able to appreciate what may be a potential problem for the client, but is of little or even no consequence to the broker.

Another important factor in managing the relationship is to encourage open and frank discussion at all levels. Surprisingly, some clients may not be as enthusiastic to voice concerns as one might imagine. Therefore, whilst the feedback from the team members and account managers is essential, it is still also important that the senior managers periodically meet with their counterparts at the client and encourage discussion of any concerns.

Performance measurement and benchmarking of the service is therefore a combination of:

- management information (*MI*) generated by workflow analysis;
- feedback from the client team;
- feedback from periodic senior manager–client liaison meetings;
- internal feedback across the organisation.

The collation of the information, assessment and action in response to a client problem must take place on a regular, possibly daily, basis and must be discussed with other client facing areas in the organisation. It has already been noted that it is doubtful that the client will have only one relationship with the organisation, and to ignore the relationships with other areas is foolhardy to say the least. Larger clients will probably look at the whole relationship with the counterpart – quite likely on a global basis – so, feedback must be on a similar basis. It is important from a risk management point of view to share information and compare situations with respect to a counterpart.

It is just as important to do so from the client service viewpoint because client service and customer relationship management is a team effort.

ESCALATION PROCEDURES

It is vital that the manager establishes a procedure whereby all issues are reported and documented and that appropriate action is signed off. This may well be by maintaining a client log or something similar.

Issues that will be included in such a log would be:

- complaints;
- errors;
- failure to meet benchmark standard;
- regulatory or legal issues.

Action will range from written communication through to arranging a client meeting if the issue is serious. There may equally be a no-action decision. By establishing the client log as a discipline in the team, the manager has every chance to pre-empt and prevent problems as well as providing a proactive management and response to the client in the event of a problem or failure to meet standard levels.

To be fully effective, the client logs must be completed daily and record no-issues as well as matters that require logging. It is important to include this no-issues reporting as it can be used as a high-profile means to measure performance.

CLIENT LIAISON PROGRAMMES

The important question here is what are the liaison meetings to achieve?

Undertaking the exercise (Box 9.3) can be very worth-while in establishing what liaison is all about.

Box 9.3 Exercise.

Consider the following statements:

1. Liaison meetings are only needed when a problem has occurred.
2. Liaison meetings are to allow a preamble before some kind of corporate entertaining.
3. Liaison meetings are to enable the broker to make a presentation on the developments to the services.
4. Liaison meetings are an informal opportunity to discuss issues.

Decide which of these statements you most agree with and then prepare an objective list (internal use) and an agenda (to be sent to the client) for such a meeting.

Source: the**dsc**.portfolio.

By undertaking this exercise the importance of planning liaison meetings can be understood. Going to visit the client for an informal chat can have merits, but by and large the liaison meeting will only be productive if there are clear objectives and both groups have had time to prepare.

FRONT-OFFICE CLIENT TEAM

Any client liaison programme will need to be worked out with reference to the internal co-operation and relationship with the sales desk. Simple co-ordination of client meetings and information can be supplemented by regular meetings to discuss the client's activities and feedback.

The successful development of the relationship with the client is conditional on the development of the relationship between operations and the internal sales desk team.

INDUSTRY ISSUES

Understanding the client's business is essential to providing the kind of service the client will benefit from and appreciate. The manager needs to create an environment where awareness of developments in the industry – and, in particular, those that will have a significant impact on the client base – is standard. This may be easy to set as an objective, but how is it achievable?

In general terms, it can be achieved through:

- giving staff access to industry journals and websites of relevant organisations – such as exchanges – and key industry bodies – such as the International Securities

Services Association, Association of British Insurers, AUTIF, etc.;

- being members of these industry associations;
- nominating people for membership of committees and working parties.

It should be easy for the manager to recognise that the ability of team members at all levels to discuss business issues with clients counts towards creating the desired professional image.

TRAINING THE TEAM

It is an inescapable fact that there is a constant need for training in client teams. This training encompasses not only relevant business skills but also personal skills such as languages and presentation.

Part of the manager's role will be to establish co-ordinated structured training programmes for client facing teams based on the client base, products used, industry changes, use of technology and regulation.

ANALYSING COMPETITION

Clients will inevitably make comparisons between the services available from brokers. They will analyse the latest developments in technology-based services, costs and innovative services such as pricing and valuations. The manager must be prepared to establish a process to provide continuous monitoring of the market place, both domestically and internationally. This monitoring will feed into the ongoing development of the services.

DEVELOPING THE SERVICE

There can be a danger that a client team is set up with adequate resource, good levels of activity from quality clients and suitable procedures. Then, business expands, more clients are obtained, their demands increase and the service is under pressure. This, if not managed, leads to problems, reputation damage and, ultimately, loss of business. It is perhaps an obvious observation, and yet it can happen quickly if there is no planning and development of the service by the manager.

One way of achieving this is by creating a business plan for the service encompassing:

- products to be offered;
- products to be developed;
- personnel development;
- technology development;
- client business awareness;
- relationship management;
- performance measurement.

Such plans should cover the short, medium and long term and should not be a wish list, but a carefully thought out plan including costs, revenue and risk management analysis.

WHAT ARE THE POTENTIAL PROBLEMS IN CUSTOMER RELATIONSHIPS?

There are numerous potential problems ranging from minor issues to full-blown complaints. Identifying and dealing with each is the key to successful relationship management. If we assume that problems will fall into various categories we might come up with a matrix like the one shown in Table 9.1.

Table 9.1

Category	Probable source or cause
Incorrect data	System problems, human error
Delayed data	System problems
Late settlement	Incorrect instructions
Missed corporate actions	Human error
Failure to respond to query	Human error
Argument over process or procedure	Personality clash
Interest claim	Delayed settlement/incorrect data
Problems with give-ups	Poor communication/human error

Source: the**dsc**.portfolio.

Any of the above can be minor or major issues and can occur because of either the broker or the client or both. It may also be the fault of an agent (internal/external) – such as custodians, clearing agents or executing brokers.

Clearly, the provision of clearing and prime brokerage services offers scope for problems, particularly as they are heavily dependent on good communication. Another major issue to be faced is the potential for a personality clash, although in the latter case active management of the client team should avoid an account manager being unsuited to the client.

Undoubtedly, communication is often at the heart of many problems. It may be internally or externally or both that the breakdown occurs. Either way it needs to be stressed to the team that communication is vitally important to the efficient operation of the service.

The timing of any response is also vital. It is quite possible to pre-empt an issue becoming a problem simply by advising the client if, for example, a system problem is likely to delay data.

MANAGING RISK IN THE CUSTOMER RELATIONSHIP

Whilst the provision of a high-quality client service is the objective of the team, doing so in a controlled manner is the overriding goal. It is not good enough to take decisions on matters with a view to not upsetting the client if the decision is creating unacceptable risk to the firm. Avoiding unnecessary and contentious actions is fine only if there is no inherent risk, and if there may be a risk, that action is cleared at the highest level.

The manager has the responsibility for maintaining a

good working relationship with the client in an environment that reflects the regulatory requirements and risk parameters of the organisation. Offering client services like third-party clearing is exposing the organisation to certain risks over and above that for its normal business. It is important to accept that client business is a counterparty risk and any added value services offered as part of the client package are increasing that risk.

The controls and procedures put in place by the manager to protect the organisation from such risk must form the basis of the customer relationship. Only in very exceptional cases, or if there is realistically little or no risk in waiving a control, can such a decision be acceptable. A client putting pressure on the broker to waive those controls in any other circumstance is unacceptable, whoever that client may be.

Likewise, client service personnel cannot have the authority to waive controls and the manager should only authorise such a decision after first clearing it with the group risk managers. If enforcing the procedure means that a client moves elsewhere, then that is a risk the manager must take after fully consulting with the client, the sales desk and the senior risk manager. Consider the following potential situations:

1. Client fails to pay a derivative margin call on due day and due day +1, citing problems at the custodian, but says they will definitely settle tomorrow.
2. Client fails to sign and return swap confirmation sent out 10 days ago.

3. Client needs to withdraw a maturing treasury bill that is being used as collateral and promises to replace it with a new one next day.
4. Client cannot provide the booking for a trade as the fund managers have not completed the order.

Each of these situations has a different risk level, but all are not satisfactory. The team members dealing with these scenarios really should refer each to the manager as they can quickly escalate and may need higher level decisions, such as cancellation of the trade.

CLIENT VISITS

Earlier in the chapter we looked at the client liaison visit and the objectives such a visit should have and also saw how other important issues surround communication with the sales desk and other client groups within the organisation over planned visits.

It hardly inspires a positive image when the client receives two visits, sales desk and operations, on the same day from the same counterpart. This is particularly the case if the two broker teams are not aware that the other is visiting the client.

The bottom line here is that the managers should ensure that client visits are undertaken with due diligence on planning and co-ordination and that they are undertaken in a professional way that enhances, not damages, the firm's reputation.

Successfully managing the client facing areas depends on the choice of people, the policy on the services, products and support provided, and the constant monitoring of performance, industry initiatives and developments, and changes to the business profiles of individual clients. Years of building reputation and creditability can be destroyed in a very short space of time. The managers must convey this to the whole team and make it especially clear to the client services team that they are nothing without the support and skills of the rest of the organisation. Likewise, a good support team is wasted if the client service team cannot retain and gain new clients.

Building a successful customer-orientated operations team takes patience and often considerable tact. It needs to be managed and developed with drive and innovation allied to discipline and attention to detail. Over-selling the services will lead to problems but under-resourcing the structure will also cause problems. Failure to have adequate procedures and controls and to oversee the relationship management will be disastrous.

It is worth repeating the quote at the beginning of this chapter:

Developing and managing a successful client facing product is an art not an exact science; years of building the successful product will involve teams of people and yet it can be undone by a moment of indiscipline or madness by a single person.

David Loader

Chapter

10

....

MANAGEMENT INFORMATION

Being a manager is about making decisions, being a successful manager is about making informed decisions.

David Loader

Is management information (*MI*) of assistance or a hindrance?

MI data is time-consuming to produce and goes out-of-date quickly, but without data on key aspects of the operations function the manager cannot manage.

But, what is MI and why and how is it used?

Information can be critical, important or used periodically. Broken down further, there is information that is about the current situation within the function, information about the possible future and the definitive past situations in the function, and information about trends that are occurring in the function. There are data on people, overall performance, costs, volume of business, system performance, counterparty performance, reconciliations and problems.

Much of the data produced have a dual purpose. They are used by the operations team itself and also by management groups, including business managers. There is also the need to produce information for external consumption, and this may well be drawn from the same source as the MI. Not surprisingly this becomes a complex scenario that often requires systems to manage the MI, and so we have management information systems (MISs).

What does the operations manager actually need in the way of information and what information is needed by the business managers and others?

The role of the operations manager has been described

earlier in the book. It revolves around managing the day-to-day performance of the function, managing change and developing the capability and resource. Clearly, this requires information if the manager is to be able to make comparisons, identify trends, and develop procedures and resource. Planning is a significant part of the role, and the process of planning needs historical data as well as data on projected growth.

Fundamental data about the operations function will include:

- activity;
- errors;
- settlement performance;
- costs;
- client complaints;
- counterparty claims;
- claims made to counterparties;
- operational risk status.

This may seem simple, and it is as long as two basic principles are observed.

First, the data must be accurate and up to date. Second, its production must be justified.

All too often the production of MI degenerates into copious amounts of data that are either irrelevant or basically unusable. As the production, collation and distribution of these data is not cheap, despite assumptions that – as they are system-generated – they cost little to produce, they represent a significant and unnecessary operations cost.

Too much data can actually increase operational risk, as critically important information gets lost in the mass of data being churned out. The challenge to the operations manager is to identify the precise data that are needed, when they are required, how they will be produced, what quality assurance can be applied and, finally, how they are to be used and distributed.

From this the manager can produce information paths which – once identified and in place – will streamline the process of producing MI and make the data produced and distributed relevant.

INFORMATION PATHS

The principle behind information paths can be illustrated by Figure 10.1.

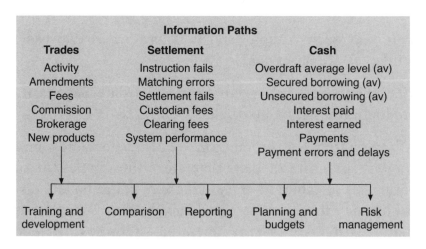

Figure 10.1 Information paths.

Source: the**dsc**.portfolio.

From Figure 10.1 it can be seen how the information is sourced from three main categories of data and then fed through into five specific areas. The information is not provided universally, but rather by validation of request.

Validating the request is vitally important. Many firms have highly confidential information about clients, products, exposures and payment instructions. Whilst trading activity might be used in all five specific areas shown, average overdraft levels are unlikely to be directly relevant to training and development. Any request for statistics and data must be approved at senior level and not just provided if asked for. Very often, elements of fraud and criminal activity are enhanced by the ability to obtain access to information about activity, business and client profiles, and anything to do with payments.

The data used in comparison processes are drawn from all three main sources, but the manager must realise that – once the process of comparison has taken place – the findings are highly sensitive and are not for general distribution.

For each type and size of firm the sources and extent of the information used will vary.

DISTRIBUTION

The distribution of the data is governed by the need-to-know principle.

Distribution can be real time, daily, periodic or *ad hoc*. Some data will be distributed in standard format and other data in a specified format, and data may be for internal or external consumption, or both. In the latter case, data supplied externally may be different from that distributed internally.

MI is either produced by areas and fed into a central MI unit, or just compiled and provided by a business area. Either way the validation of the request for the data and the distribution of the data is a key risk control, and procedures must be developed to ensure this control happens. Most MI is transferred through systems, although some hard copy reporting is done.

Requests for information may be continuous – for instance, it is not unreasonable for the risk management team to require significant amounts of information on positions, cash movements and funding. This may be the raw data or the data after they have been processed through the comparison analysis.

Either way we come back to the underlying issue of credibility of the data produced.

MI PRODUCTION

The manager is required to put in place procedures to authenticate the MI before it is distributed to other parties or used by the manager. Naturally, this will involve making personnel aware of the importance of accuracy and timeliness of the processes and tasks they perform.

It will also need elements of quality assurance to ensure the credibility of the output. As MI will often be used in preparing external regulatory and client reporting, the standard of the MI produced is both imperative and also a public benchmark of the quality of the whole operations function. Error-strewn MI is useless, expensive and will damage reputation. It is also highly dangerous when used in risk and planning.

The three stages in MI production are:

1. Sourcing data.
2. Collation and validation.
3. Production.

SOURCING DATA

The sourcing of the data will be decided by the type of data, frequency of capture and source of the data – i.e., system or manual collation. Most MI systems will have standard parameters and built-in prompts for source and data capture. Bespoke data may need to be collated from several sources including non-system and external sources. This would include exchange fees and brokerage that may be received via invoices and then input to internal systems (Figure 10.2). Timing becomes an issue

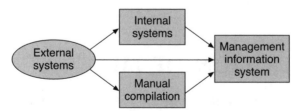

Figure 10.2 Sources of MI.

here. Monthly brokerage information cannot be produced until brokerage invoices have been received. This is compounded by the fact that some exchanges and custodians have automated brokerage and fee services where data for the preceding period are immediately available. In this case the manager may consider incorporating estimated amounts, but this must be clearly noted in any reports produced.

COMPILATION AND VALIDATION

As mentioned above the precise process of compilation of MI will depend on the business and the information requirements. The critically important thing is not the quantity but the quality of data. Vast MISs may be impressive, but are probably useless. Compact, clear and relevant MI is a bonus to the managers and the business.

Compiling data in this way is not a part-time occupation. The objectives must be understood if first-class information is to be compiled and so, too, must the importance of accuracy and timing. However well put together and comprehensive the MI might be, it is of little value if it arrives late. Incorrect MI is a disaster.

PRODUCTION OF MI

MI itself falls into different classifications, and again the need for the compiler to understand the user's need is crucial. In principle the MI will be used for one or more of the areas shown in Figure 10.1. These were:

- training and development;
- comparison;
- reporting;
- risk management;
- planning and budgets.

The manager may need several different reports reflecting different ways of viewing the particular information. This is vitally important: all statistics and data are snapshots which can give a misleading message. Often, there needs to be some kind of comparison or, failing that, a note that qualifies the information.

For instance, the training logs of team members viewed at a particular point may not reflect the fact that other factors – such as heavy activity – have temporarily influenced the progress of the individual's Training and Development (T&D) programme.

Likewise, the trading activity itself – even when compared with figures for, say, the previous year – does not tell the full story. What is relevant to the operations manager is how the team dealt with the activity. Higher volumes do not have to mean higher error rates (in fact, the opposite can apply as individuals tend to concentrate more in heavy activity), and the net settlement cost of a transaction may well come down in an efficient operations function that experiences growth in activity. The manager needs data that will tell them how the operations function is reacting. They also need data to enable them to plan ahead and to take action when the MI is telling them things are changing, like the performance.

MI is produced from central systems, operations systems, the manager's PC and sometimes manually. Certainly, the manager may merge data from different centrally generated or team-produced standards such as reports to suit their own requirements. Also, some MI – like staff appraisals, T&D programme and client correspondence – may be better kept in a manual form, at least by the manager. Comparisons will often be about benchmarking, so some MI is about targets and standards and can be highly confidential. Other MI – such as trends – may be information that the manager can utilise to praise or chastise the team, but once again it is important to stress that the use of data cannot be selective such that an incorrect or confused picture is provided.

Consider the impact of presenting data to the team that are quickly seen to be flawed. Why should anyone give any credibility to future data? Data should be given straight. If they're bad, they're bad; if they're good, they're good. Operations managers may feel as if they are at the centre of politics sometimes. In some firms the use of spin to provide an enhanced image may be common, but most people see right through the spin so that little is gained in the long term and there is much to lose by massaging MI.

RISKS IN MI

There is clearly operational risk in MI.

Incorrect data are the obvious risk, particularly if the data are used in key decision making or analysis like risk management. Likewise, the manager must be aware of the regulatory reporting that is associated with data produced from MI systems, and the dangers of late, wrongly calculated or incorrect filing of these data.

The robustness of the internal procedures in the operational processes will underpin the quality of the MI sources whilst the manager's control and monitoring of external counterparts that contribute data to MI is also crucially important.

One only needs to consider why internal MI did not help to highlight increasing problems at many organisations that have suffered disasters. Quality MI would have indicated that the use of cash was not being justified by the trading activities and positions apparently showing in the books and records. The answer in most cases is almost certainly that the MI is either poor, too comprehensive and lacking credibility, or was good but that managers did not comprehend the message that it was sending.

Either way there is an operational risk because there is an assumption that MI is contributing positively to risk control.

The major risk associated with MI is that it is inherently difficult to manage. Too often, there are unrealistic demands for unnecessary and unused information, without consideration for the logistics and costs of producing the information. This is compounded by a lack of real objectives for its use.

Information and communication in the financial services industry is crucial, and yet here we have a specific information gathering and distribution process that all too often lacks focus.

Whatever the task facing an operations manager, having the background knowledge of what is happening, how it's happening, what it is costing, how things are impacting and whether the performance is improving or worsening is vital if a professional decision is to be made.

It is down to the operations manager to decide what they need from MI as well as contributing to what others need. Ask yourself these questions:

- What is the information that will help me understand the status of the operations function?
- What information will help me benchmark performance?
- What information do I need to prepare budgets?
- What information do I need to manage projects?
- What information do I need to develop the team?
- What information do I need to help me manage risk?

Once you have done that, ask yourself the million dollar question:

- What information don't I need?

You may find the first six questions easier than the last, but it is imperative that the manager takes tough decisions and cuts out unnecessary data. This will make the MI that is produced much more productive and beneficial to the manager.

Lack of any MI, poor MI and abuse of MI are all severe weaknesses to the firm and a problem, sooner or later, for the manager. In contrast, quality MI helps the business and the manager more than they may realise. We have talked about managing change and the operations manager's role in managing risk elsewhere in this book. How can this be achieved without the support of quality data on the past and present and projections for the future state of the operations function?

History is full of examples of those who had tremendous success because of the quality and timeliness of vital information, but it is also littered with examples of those who suffered because they had no such information.

In the unrelenting pressure on operations teams in financial markets, information or lack of it is the fine line between a manager's success and failure.

Chapter

11

....

OUTSOURCING/ INSOURCING OPERATIONS FUNCTIONS

OUTSOURCING

There is nothing new about outsourcing or insourcing operations functions. It has been part of technology management for decades, and the use of an independent custodian or fund administrator is hardly new in the securities trading or fund management world.

Outsourcing is a common enough business consideration and we often hear senior executives explaining an out-source decision as 'returning to our core activity'. In most of these cases they are referring to operations functions that it is deemed can be better resourced and developed externally than internally as they are not part of the sharp end of the business – in other words, they are a cost centre rather than a profit centre.

Of course, in many organisations the reverse is the case and the operational capability is a profit/revenue genera-tor, global or centralised clearing of derivatives being an example.

The case for outsourcing is often about cost savings, real or imagined. But there are also other very important factors to consider.

Box 11.1

In October 2005 Fred Francis, vice president, securities finance and global products for RBC Global Services, Institutional & Investor Services in an article entitled 'Reducing the admin burden' published in *FTMandate* (www.ftmandate.com) wrote:

The transactional model, where the institution segregates and decouples the FX execution from the settlement process, makes a number of assumptions: that the heightened risks of segregating FX from the settlement value chain is understood and effectively managed and mitigated; that all buyers have access to all the information they need to ascertain timing and frequency of FX execution to ensure matching of trades and value dates, that buyers have effective systems and staff competency to manage the accuracy, completeness, and performance of FX.

This model requires the institution to prove the level of performance it achieves, as well as reporting on management and demonstrating efficient governance. The requirement to keep up with increasingly complex and diverse markets, trading volatility, governance demands and the need for performance is obviously placing additional administrative and reporting burdens upon institutions.

The administrative burden and the ability to successfully manage performance levels including managing operational risk are becoming very significant. Changes to the regulatory environment – particularly where greater and more diverse use of products is being sanctioned, such as the EU Directive on UCITS and the use of derivatives – is increasing the pressure on the operations function to be able to understand, process and control the support to the trading activity in them.

However, the case for simply transferring the risk to another entity is not one that is an option. For instance, the Bank for International Settlements in its recommendations for central clearing counterparties (CCPs) stated (Box 11.2):

Box 11.2

Outsourcing assessment: CCPs can inadvertently increase their operational risk by transferring critical functions to third parties. The consultation paper states that operators should ensure that outsourced operations meet the same standards as if they were provided directly.

The Committee on Payment and Settlement Systems and the Technical Committee of the International Organization of Securities Commissions collaborated in finalizing the paper, *Recommendations for Central Counterparties*. The Authors are seeking comment by June 9th, 2004.

The outsource decision, then, must be made with due diligence in assessing not only the financial merits of the process but also the governance and performance merits.

REGULATION AND OUTSOURCING

What is the position on outsourcing from the regulatory viewpoint. The Bank for International Settlement (*BIS*) Basel Committee on Banking Supervision published a document entitled *Outsourcing in Financial Services*. An extract is given in Box 11.3 including a definition of outsourcing.

Box 11.3

1. Executive summary

Financial services businesses throughout the world are increasingly using third parties to carry out activities that the businesses themselves would normally have undertaken. Industry research and surveys by regulators show financial firms outsourcing significant parts of their regulated and unregulated activities. These outsourcing arrangements are also becoming increasingly complex.

Outsourcing has the potential to transfer risk, management and compliance to third parties who may not be regulated, and who may operate offshore. In these situations, how can financial service businesses remain confident that they remain in charge of their own business and in control of their business risks? How do they know they are complying with their regulatory responsibilities? How can these businesses demonstrate that they are doing so when regulators ask?

To help answer these questions and to guide regulated businesses, the Joint Forum established a working group to develop high-level principles about outsourcing. In this paper, the key issues and risks are spelt out in more detail and principles are put forward that can serve as benchmarks. The principles apply across the banking, insurance and securities sectors, and the international committees involved in each sector may build on these principles to offer more specific and focused guidance. Selected international case studies (see Annex A*) show why these questions matter.

Today outsourcing is increasingly used as a means of both reducing costs and achieving strategic aims. Its potential impact can be seen across many business activities, including information technology (e.g., applications development, programming, and coding), specific operations (e.g., some aspects of finance and accounting, back-office activities & processing, and administration), and contract functions (e.g., call centres). Industry reports and regulatory surveys of industry practice indicate that financial firms are entering into arrangements in which other firms – related firms within a corporate group and third-party service providers – conduct significant parts of the enterprise's regulated and un-regulated activities.

---

* This is in the full document available at *www.bis.org*

Activities and functions within an organisation are performed and delivered in diverse ways.

An institution might split such functions as product manufacturing, marketing, back-office and distribution within the regulated entity. Where a regulated entity keeps such arrangements inhouse, but operates some activities from various locations, this would not be classified as outsourcing. The entity would therefore be expected to provide for any risks posed by this in its regular risk management framework.

Increasingly more complex arrangements are developing whereby related entities perform some activities, while unrelated service providers perform others. In each case the service provider may or may not be a regulated entity. The Joint Forum principles are designed to apply whether or not the service provider is a regulated entity. Outsourcing has been identified in various industry and regulatory reports as raising issues related to risk transfer and management, frequently on a cross-border basis, and industry and regulators acknowledge that this increased reliance on the outsourcing of activities may impact on the ability of regulated entities to manage their risks and monitor their compliance with regulatory requirements. Additionally, there is concern among regulators as to how outsourcing potentially could impede the ability of regulated entities to demonstrate to regulators (e.g., through examinations) that they are taking appropriate steps to manage their risks and comply with applicable regulations.

Among the specific concerns raised by outsourcing activities is the potential for over-reliance on outsourced activities that are critical to the ongoing viability of a regulated entity as well as its obligations to customers.

Regulated entities can mitigate these risks by taking steps (as discussed in the principles) to:

- draw up comprehensive and clear outsourcing policies;
- establish management programmes;
- require contingency planning by the outsourcing firm;
- negotiate appropriate outsourcing contracts; and

- analyse the financial and infrastructure resources of the service provider.

Regulators can also mitigate concerns by ensuring that outsourcing is adequately considered in their assessments of individual firms whilst taking account of concentration risks in third party providers when considering systemic risk issues. Of particular interest to regulators is the preservation at the regulated entity of strong corporate governance. In this regard outsourcing activities that may impede an outsourcing firm's management from fulfilling its regulatory responsibilities are of concern to regulators.

The rapid rate of IT innovation, along with an increasing reliance on external service providers have the potential of leading to systemic problems unless appropriately constrained by a combination of market and regulatory influences.

This paper attempts to spell out these concerns in more detail and develop a set of principles that gives guidance to firms, and to regulators, to help them better mitigate these concerns without hindering the efficiency and effectiveness of firms.

2. Guiding principles – overview

The Joint Forum has developed the following high-level principles. The first seven principles cover the responsibilities of regulated entities when they outsource their activities, and the last two principles cover regulatory roles and responsibilities. Here we present an overview of the principles. More detail may be found in section 9.*

I.   A regulated entity seeking to outsource activities should have in place a comprehensive policy to guide the assessment of whether and how those activities can be appropriately outsourced. The board of directors or equivalent body retains responsibility for the outsourcing policy and related overall responsibility for activities undertaken under that policy.

---

* This is in the full document available at *www.bis.org*

II.   The regulated entity should establish a comprehensive outsourcing risk management programme to address the outsourced activities and the relationship with the service provider.

III.   The regulated entity should ensure that outsourcing arrangements neither diminish its ability to fulfil its obligations to customers and regulators, nor impede effective supervision by regulators.

IV.   The regulated entity should conduct appropriate due diligence in selecting third-party service providers.

V.   Outsourcing relationships should be governed by written contracts that clearly describe all material aspects of the outsourcing arrangement, including the rights, responsibilities and expectations of all parties.

VI.   The regulated entity and its service providers should establish and maintain contingency plans, including a plan for disaster recovery and periodic testing of backup facilities.

VII.   The regulated entity should take appropriate steps to require that service providers protect confidential information of both the regulated entity and its clients from intentional or inadvertent disclosure to unauthorised persons.

VIII. Regulators should take into account outsourcing activities as an integral part of their ongoing assessment of the regulated entity. Regulators should assure themselves by appropriate means that any outsourcing arrangements do not hamper the ability of a regulated entity to meet its regulatory requirements.

IX.   Regulators should be aware of the potential risks posed where the outsourced activities of multiple regulated entities are concentrated within a limited number of service providers.

3. Definition

Outsourcing is defined in this paper as a regulated entity's use of a third party (either an affiliated entity within a corporate group or an entity that is external to the corporate group) to perform activities on a continuing basis that would normally be undertaken by the regulated entity, now or in the future.

Outsourcing can be the initial transfer of an activity (or a part of that activity) from a regulated entity to a third party or the further transfer of an activity (or a part thereof) from one third-party service provider to another, sometimes referred to as 'sub-contracting.' In some jurisdictions, the initial outsourcing is also referred to as subcontracting.

Firms should consider several factors as they apply these principles to activities that fall under the outsourcing definition. First, these principles should be applied according to the degree of materiality of the outsourced activity to the firm's business. Even where the activity is not material, the outsourcing entity should consider the appropriateness of applying the principles. Second, firms should consider any affiliation or other relationship between the outsourcing entity and the service provider. While it is necessary to apply the Outsourcing Principles to affiliated entities, it may be appropriate to adopt them with some modification to account for the potential for differing degrees of risk with respect to intra-group outsourcing.

Third, the firm may consider whether the service provider is a regulated entity subject to independent supervision.

According to this definition, outsourcing would not cover purchasing contracts, although as with outsourcing, firms should ensure that what they are buying is appropriate for the intended purpose. Purchasing is defined, *inter alia*, as the acquisition from a vendor of services, goods or facilities without the transfer of the purchasing firm's non-public proprietary information pertaining to its customers or other information connected with its business activities.

This paper will refer to a regulated entity as the body that is authorised for a regulated activity by a regulator. The principles set forth in this paper are targeted at such entities.

Third party or service provider refers to the entity that is undertaking the outsourced activity on behalf of the regulated entity.

The term regulator refers to all supervisory and regulatory authorities that authorise firms to undertake any regulated activity and supervise that activity.

Source: BIS.

The full document can be accessed at the BIS website *www.bis.org*

What conclusions can we draw about outsourcing?

The first and perhaps obvious conclusion is that managers must be fully involved in the process of analysing the rationale for a possible outsource and also in the outsource project should it go ahead.

In some outsource processes, notably where a fund management company outsources the bulk of the operations process to another entity, the existing operations personnel may be part of the outsource package. This is a fundamentally important issue for several reasons, not least the welfare of the individuals.

The operations team transferring to the insourcing entity has the advantage of seamlessly incorporating the 'in-house' business knowledge on processes, relationships, counterparties, etc., which is vital for continuity and maintenance of the client service. It also means that there is less impact in terms of human resources issues, as redundancies are a less likely outcome of the decision.

Second, the Request For Proposal (*RFP*) process becomes vital, and if we are to comply with the recommendations alluded to above we need to make sure the questions and analysis of the response are appropriate to allow a real assessment of the impact, including the change to the operational risk profile of the outsource to be understood.

Outsourcing some or all operations functions is more

realistic today given the greater degree of automation in the clearing and settlement processes. Focusing resource of client service delivery and risk management rather than process work is potentially more productive for just about any business, but there is another crucially important issue that the managers need to be aware of.

We can outsource functions, but not responsibility.

Returning to the BIS document, the following extract (Table 11.1) gives an illustration of the key risks involved in outsourcing.

Table 11.1 Some key risks in outsourcing – risk major concerns.

Strategic risk	The third party may conduct activities on its own behalf which are inconsistent with the overall strategic goals of the regulated entity.
	Failure to implement appropriate oversight of the outsource provider.
	Inadequate expertise to oversee the service provider.
Reputation risk	Poor service from third party.
	Customer interaction is not consistent with overall standards of the regulated entity.
	Third-party practices not in line with stated practices (ethical or otherwise) of regulated entity.
Compliance risk	Privacy laws are not complied with.
	Consumer and prudential laws not adequately complied with.
	Outsource provider has inadequate compliance systems and controls.
Operational risk	Technology failure.
	Inadequate financial capacity to fulfil obligations and/or provide remedies.
	Fraud or error.
	Risk that firms find it difficult/costly to undertake inspections.

Table 11.1 Some key risks in outsourcing (*cont.*)

Exit strategy risk	The risk that appropriate exit strategies are not in place. This could arise from overreliance on one firm, the loss of relevant skills in the institution
Exit strategy risk (*cont.*)	itself preventing it bringing the activity back in-house and contracts which make a speedy exit prohibitively expensive. Limited ability to return services to home country due to lack of staff or loss of intellectual history.
Counterparty risk	Inappropriate underwriting or credit assessments. Quality of receivables may diminish.
Country risk	Political, social and legal climate may create added risk. Business continuity planning is more complex.
Contractual risk	Ability to enforce contract. For offshoring, choice of law is important.
Access risk	Outsourcing arrangement hinders ability of regulated entity to provide timely data and other information to regulators. Additional layer of difficulty in regulator understanding activities of the outsource provider.
Concentration and systemic risk	Overall industry has significant exposure to outsource provider. This concentration risk has a number of facets, including: • Lack of control of individual firms over provider; and • Systemic risk to industry as a whole.

Service Level Agreements, contracts and penalties for non-performance will naturally be in place and offer some financial protection; however, they do not protect against damage to the firm's reputation nor to action by the regulator.

INSOURCING

The reasons behind an organisation offering insourcing are usually about the ability to make maximum use of infrastructure, particularly technology.

Consolidation in the industry can also be a factor; so, for instance, in custody we have seen a reduction in the number of organisations offering services and, at the same time, more clients seeking to outsource some or all the operations functions. The economies of scale are naturally significant for these remaining organisations and, as we noted above, with personnel transference also being a factor in most cases the taking on of additional business becomes attractive financially and logistically.

For the operations managers in these insourcing firms the general management issues – like workflow, resourcing/people issues, technology development, service delivery, etc. – are there and simply magnified by the volume processed and size of the business.

In fund administration there is perhaps greater concern about issues that arise from insourcing business. With considerable growth in the number of hedge funds, locations – such as Dublin – have seen huge increases in the number of clients the administration firms are servicing, and, at the same time, in the requirement to increase headcount to support this increased activity. As the business profile changes there are obviously issues, including risk management, third-party suppliers, and regulatory as well as human resource issues of recruitment and retention of key staff.

In addition, there is a need to be able to answer ever more comprehensive and detailed RFPs from prospective clients and an ability to demonstrate commitment to the business and the investment, particularly for technology, that is needed.

Operations managers in insourcing firms must pay very close attention to the performance of service delivery. There are more players in insourcing than popularly believed and it is certainly highly competitive, particularly with the offshoring alternatives available from amongst others India.

Risk management is also an issue and any manager with experience of running an insourcing operation will tell you that creating too much of a bespoke service facility can have massive implications for the long-term profitability of the business.

Outsource and insource offer great possibilities for cost saving and revenue generation, they also create significant changes to risk profiles and pressures on operations infrastructure. Both can be considered but neither is necessarily going to deliver the expected outcome.

Chapter

12

....

INDUSTRY DEVELOPMENTS

If you don't know where you're going, you'll end up somewhere else.

Yogi Berra

The industry is undergoing significant and constant change. Operations managers are at the forefront of dealing with the implications of this change, and it represents a very significant challenge.

Change, of course, is nothing new and, indeed, the operations function has had many highly important and major changes to deal with such as, for instance, increasing use of technology in processes, the move to dematerialised settlement, cross-border trading, the introduction of financial derivatives, the Y2K issues, the introduction of the euro and change to the regulatory environment. The changing structure of the industry itself (the rise and fall of Internet trading, exchange and clearing house mergers and the evolution of the mega-investment banks) has also presented challenges to operations managers.

Of all the major global issues the move towards straight-through-processing (STP) and dealing with operational risk have probably presented some of the biggest challenges and involved operations managers and teams in very significant projects, the successful outcome of which has been crucial to their businesses.

Exchanges and clearing organisations have moved forward in response to market pressures, with electronic trading replacing open-outcry in many markets and consolidated clearing, depository and custodial-type functions occurring, for example, in Germany and latterly within the Euronext environment where Clearnet, LCH, CREST and Euroclear are or will be linked. In custody the pressures on businesses to enhance technology has proved too costly, and so mergers and firms ceasing to offer the service has resulted in a significant shift towards a few major players.

Not all of the change has been totally successful. The idea that there was a huge demand by retail customers for access to markets and products, fuelled by increasing wealth and the booming equity markets (particularly the dotcom companies), led to the establishing of new and specialised markets such as the Neuer Markt by Deutsche Börse in Frankfurt and Jiway by Sweden's OM and Morgan Stanley. Today, just a few years later and after considerable investment, both of these markets have closed.

The whole structure of clearing and settlement is itself being altered by the central clearing counterparty (*CCP*) concept, remote clearing, the clearing of products like repos and swaps that have traditionally settled on a counterparty to counterparty basis and by the introduction of netting and products like Continuous Linked Settlement (*CLS*) in foreign exchange.

Each of these changes results in a significant project for the operations managers and teams that will encompass technology, procedures, re-engineering operations, re-training and new pressures.

Managing the changes and, indeed, anticipating changes is a critical part of the manager's role; so, what are the really major changes happening today and those that will happen in the future?

The following extracts from organisations and a look at the output from industry bodies can perhaps provide an insight.

We can look first at the corporate statement about the CRESTCo/Euroclear merger (Box 12.1).

Box 12.1   Euroclear/CRESTCo merger.

With the announcement of their merger, CRESTCo and Euroclear together are putting forward a new vision and a new model for European settlement. We intend to cut away the current costs and complexity of cross-border settlement by removing borders. We intend to create a single domestic settlement space covering the five countries in the NewGroup – Belgium, France, Ireland, the Netherlands and the United Kingdom ...

The corner stones of this programme are choice, customer focus and credibility.

Source: CRESTCo/Euroclear *Delivering a Domestic Market in Europe* published July 2002.

Cross-border transactions are not new, but an age-old problem has been the costs and risks involved in settling business transacted in another market. On the face of it, this merger would seem, like the concept behind Clearstream, to address those issues. For the operations manager the issues are technology, re-engineering and re-training so that the advantages the merger is designed to deliver can be utilised. Will the clearing and settlement rationalisation lead Europe to have two large and sophisticated groupings? What will happen if the 'New-Group' and Clearstream decide to merge too? Will the near monopoly situation be good for the market? What does it mean for technology?

These are important questions and, clearly, the operations manager must remain informed on the situation as it unfolds.

What about mergers of exchanges? We can look at the corporate statement given by the Stock Exchange of Hong Kong Ltd, the Hong Kong Futures Exchange Ltd and Hong Kong Securities Clearing Company Ltd (Box 12.2).

Box 12.2   About HKEx – company profile – basics of the new organisation.

Powerful forces in the financial services industry and the financial markets are combining to meet the needs of all participants.

HKEx is the holding company of The Stock Exchange of Hong Kong Limited, Hong Kong Futures Exchange Limited and Hong Kong Securities Clearing Company Limited. It brings together the market organisations which have transformed Hong Kong's financial services industry from a domestically focused industry to the global player it is today.

HKEx went public in June 2000 following the integration of the securities and futures market. As a listed company, answerable to its shareholders, HKEx competes vigorously for opportunities in the region and around the world. It is a market-driven business, operating business-driven markets.

HKEx is having an effective commercial business structure, geared to achieving growth and continuing success. Its operations are organised into focused and commercially driven business units, directly supervised and controlled by HKEx's management and board. The board, HKEx's highest decision-making body, shapes policies for major strategic and operational matters.

HKEx provides a comprehensive range of pre- and post-trade investment services. Business units have been established in four functions, comprising the exchange unit, the clearing unit, the e-business and information services unit, and the IT/systems unit.

Source: HKEx website *www.hkex.com.hk*

The commercial rationale for the creation of this grouping is reasonably easy to understand, and indeed other groupings have happened such as SGX in Singapore and, on a wider scale, Euronext in Europe. Has it benefited businesses from an operations point of view?

Anything that reduces the number of counterparties that an operations function needs to deal with does, on the face of it, have benefits. Merging securities and derivatives markets and clearing achieves this, but the real benefits are actually in the ability to provide central clearing, netting of settlement and offsetting of the positions for margin purposes as these reduce both risk and costs.

Other major developments include those addressing risk. One such development is occurring in the foreign exchange markets (Box 12.3).

Box 12.3   CLS Bank.

In foreign exchange markets the risk associated with settlement in different time zones has been addressed by the development of Continuous Linked Settlement (CLS) by CLS Bank. Here, the concepts behind central clearing are incorporated into the settlement of transactions, removing the so-called Herstatt risk whereby an unfortunate bank in the US found that between transferring deutschmarks in Frankfurt and receiving dollars in New York, Herstatt Bank went bust.

The outcome operationally is a change in settlement procedure (margin, collateral, etc.) in return for greater risk management in what has hitherto been a potential high-risk area. CLS is a payment versus payment mechanism where it effectively becomes the FX central counterparty.

CLS commenced in Q4 2002.

REGULATORY CHANGES AND T&C

Any regulatory change can impact in many ways on operations, but competency is a particularly important one.

Many firms, as a matter of course, will actively encourage and may make mandatory personnel development through a variety of training mediums. Increasingly, there are both regulatory and commercial reasons for firms in all areas of the financial markets to ensure that their operations and support personnel are adequately trained and in possession of relevant qualifications.

Training and competency should be supported and encouraged by operations managers. But, it can and does present the manager with many problems. Budgets and time are often an issue, but so too is the need to recruit and retain qualified staff in a relatively competitive market place. The regulatory pressure in some jurisdictions adds to the problem, and often the manager is left with a deadline to meet and little scope to meet it.

Planning a training and development (*T&D*) programme and sticking to it, come what may, is part of the solution. Getting the necessary budget is another, and here the operations manager needs to use arguments that revolve around and emphasise regulation and risk management.

INDUSTRY RECOMMENDATION

There are recommendations like those published by the International Securities Services Association (*ISSA*) and Group of Thirty (*G30*). These may or may not have a major impact, depending on the firm and where it is located, but as industry awareness is important from a client service point of view, all operations managers should familiarise themselves with such recommendations.

SHORTENING SETTLEMENT CYCLES

The drive towards $T + 1$ settlement in equity securities has somewhat slowed recently for many good reasons. More CCP and the aftermath of September 11 combined with a fall in the equity market leading to lower volumes and less mergers and acquisitions (*M&A*) activity have all served to focus attention elsewhere.

The introduction of $T + 1$ may well be on the back

burner, but it is still very much alive, contrary to comments from some quarters. As STP becomes a reality through significant changes in the market and clearing structures, the foundation for a successful migration to $T + 0$ becomes a reality and $T + 1$ a certainty.

It seems obvious that in an industry where there are globalised businesses – such as banks, brokers and fund managers trading multi-products, multi-currency and often linked product trades like buy/writes in options, for instance – a uniform settlement cycle is simply imperative. $T + 1$ for bonds and most exchange traded derivatives, $T + 3$ or 2 or 5 for equities and corporate bonds and 2-day spot FX is unacceptable.

Operations managers need to be aware of the ultimate goal of CCP and $T + 1$.

WHAT ELSE?

Many other organisations are heavily involved in the changes that are happening in the industry. We have already mentioned some of them in the book, and others the manager should be aware of will be included in the following subsections.

Bank for International Settlement

In particular, the operations managers need to be aware of Basel II in respect of operational risk (visit *www.bis.org*, see also Appendix C).

Securities Industry Association

The Securities Industry Association (*SIA*) is a US-based organisation that was established in 1972 through the merger of the Association of Stock Exchange Firms (1913) and the Investment Bankers' Association (1912).

The SIA brings together the shared interests of more than 600 securities firms to accomplish common goals. SIA member firms (including investment banks, broker-dealers, and mutual fund companies) are active in all US and foreign markets and in all phases of corporate and public finance. The US securities industry manages the accounts of nearly 93 million investors directly and indirectly through corporate, thrift and pension plans. In 2001, the industry generated $198 billion in US revenue and $358 billion in global revenues. Securities firms employ approximately 750,000 individuals in the US.

The values upon which SIA guides its members and their employees in the securities industry can be articulated as shown in Box 12.4.

Box 12.4

Recognising their fundamental role in the continued growth and development of the capital markets, as well as their responsibility to issuers and investors, SIA member firms hold these values: adherence to ethical and professional standards; commitment to the best interests of clients; and exercise of unquestioned integrity in business and personal dealings in the industry and within the firms.

SIA member firms uphold these values through responsible management; superior products and services; thorough and ongoing professional education for employees; and clear, consistent and complete information for clients about products, services and the risks and rewards associated with investing and the capital markets.

Upon this foundation, SIA pledges to earn, inspire and maintain the public's trust and confidence in the securities industry and the US capital markets.

Source: SIA *www.sia.com*

Alternative Investment Management Association

AIMA represents firms involved in sectors of the industry covering alternative investments such as hedge funds. It is a useful reference source for hedge fund activity. It has recently published a *Guide to Fund of Hedge Funds* that focuses on risk, due diligence and management. The website address is *www.aima.org*

International Swaps and Derivatives Association

ISDA (Box 12.5) is a producer of standardised documentation for over-the-counter derivatives including swaps and credit derivatives. It is the global trade association representing leading participants in the privately negotiated derivatives industry, a business which includes interest rate, currency, commodity, credit and equity swaps, as well as related products such as caps, collars, floors and swaptions.

Box 12.5

ISDA was chartered in 1985, and today numbers over 575 member institutions from 44 countries on six continents. These members include most of the world's major institutions and leading end-users who deal in privately negotiated derivatives, as well as associated service providers and consultants.

Since its inception, the Association has pioneered efforts to identify and reduce the sources of risk in the derivatives and risk management business. Among its most notable accomplishments are: developing the ISDA master agreement; publishing a wide range of related documentation materials and instruments covering a variety of transaction types; producing legal opinions on the enforceability of netting (available only to ISDA members); securing recognition of the risk-reducing effects of netting in determining capital requirements; promoting sound risk management practices; and advancing the understanding and treatment of derivatives and risk management from public policy and regulatory capital perspectives.

Source: ISDA *www.isda.org*

International Securities Markets Association

ISMA provides much useful help and guidance to members and runs the TRAX system for settlement of international securities. It is a self-regulatory organisation and trade association with a global membership. It has headquarters in Zurich and provides rules and recommendations governing trading and settlement in the international securities market including Eurobonds. The website address is *www.isma.org*

GSCS benchmarks

This is a useful source of benchmarking for settlement, safekeeping and operational risk by country updated quarterly and published by Metal Bulletin plc.

Metal Bulletin also publish several titles that will be of interest to managers. These and details of GSCS can be found at *www.metalbulletin.com*

OTHER INDUSTRY ORGANISATIONS

There are numerous industry organisations covering securities, commodities and derivatives, most of whom are involved in the ongoing evolution of the markets and clearing and settlement issues.

REMOTE CLEARING

One further development that has impacted and is impacting to a significant degree is the ability to remotely clear markets. In the traditional infrastructure, a firm that traded on a market had a physical presence there and so, naturally, the clearing and settlement function was also present. As globalisation of the markets grew, the same firm either continued to use agents or, if they had aspirations to become global investment banks, they began to create the same trading and settlement infrastructures for each market. Not surprisingly, this created many problems, not least the cost. However, just as important as the cost factor was the management issue. Having a presence in several markets created a situation where the control procedures and maintenance of common standards became difficult. In effect, a firm had several relatively autonomous functions and, whilst control was an issue, the benefits were local knowledge and local service delivery. The debate on the relative benefits and downside reached a climax following the activities of Nick Leeson at Baring's Futures in Singapore. Here, a breakdown of basic controls and management – created by the autonomy of the office – resulted in uncontrolled dealing and use of funding that ultimately caused the collapse of the bank.

Although there were many factors involved in this case, the one that continuously raises its head is the way in which the activities were not seen by the main office in London or, apparently, the regional office in Tokyo.

The difficulties with managing a global business as several mini-businesses had been illustrated and attention turned towards how effective 'global management' actually was. The benefits of the idea of centralising the clearing and settlement processes had long been known in the derivatives markets. The securities markets were different, and in some more problematic, as they involved depositories and custodians, although the advent of the CCP has changed this. This management of assets was not the real management issue; knowing what was being managed was. There were of course many reasons for potential problems: time zones, culture, language and knowledge/skills. Today, there are global firms with global management teams in place, but the fear is still that the enormity and complexity of the business is not always matched by the ability to have the necessary information, controls and management oversight. This was examined in previous chapters; undoubtedly, poor management information systems (*MIS*s) are often at the heart of inefficient and vulnerable businesses. A challenge today is for technology firms, clearing organisations and managers in firms to devise the necessary policies, systems, products and people skills to manage an increasingly complex and very fast industry. Remote clearing achieves this by allowing the process to be managed if the firm has the ability to see the data and has the expertise to interpret and manage the clearing and settlement process with the maximum cost and risk efficiency. This and many other developments are of course contributing to the realising of a true STP environment.

THE G30's 20 RECOMMENDATIONS

Creating a strengthened, interoperable global network

1. Eliminate paper and automate communication, data capture, and enrichment.

2. Harmonize messaging standards and communication protocols.

3. Develop and implement reference data standards.

4. Synchronize timing between different clearing and settlement systems and associated payment and foreign-exchange systems.

5. Automate and standardize institutional trradematching.

6. Expand the use of central counterparties.

7. Permit securities lending and borrowing to expedite settlement.

8. Automate and standardize asset servicing processes, including corporate actions, tax relief arrangements, and restrictions on foreign ownership.

Mitigating risk

9. Ensure the financial integrity of providers of clearing and settlement services.

10. Reinforce the risk management practices of users of clearing and settlement service providers.

11. Ensure final, simultaneous transfer and availability of assets.

12. Ensure effective business continuity and disaster recovery planning.

13. Address the possibility of failure of a systemically important institution.

14. Strengthen assessment of the enforceability of contracts.

15. Advance legal certainty over rights to securities, cash, or collateral.

16. Recognize and support improved valuation and closeout netting arrangements.

Improving governance

17. Ensure appointment of appropriately experienced and senior board members.

18. Promote fair access to securities clearing and settlement networks.

19. Ensure equitable and effective attention to stakeholder interests.

20. Encourage consistent regulation and oversight of securities clearing and settlement service providers.

Source: G30

Appendix

A

....

FATF DOCUMENTS ON THE FORTY RECOMMENDATIONS

INTRODUCTION

Money laundering methods and techniques change in response to developing counter-measures. In recent years, the Financial Action Task Force (*FATF*)[1] has noted increasingly sophisticated combinations of techniques, such as the increased use of legal persons to disguise the true ownership and control of illegal proceeds, and an increased use of professionals to provide advice and assistance in laundering criminal funds. These factors, combined with the experience gained through the FATF's Non-Cooperative Countries and Territories process, and a number of national and international initiatives, led the FATF to review and revise the Forty Recommendations into a new comprehensive framework for combating money laundering and terrorist financing. The FATF now calls upon all countries to take the necessary steps to bring their national systems for combating money laundering and terrorist financing into compliance with the new FATF Recommendations, and to effectively implement these measures.

The review process for revising the Forty Recommendations was an extensive one, open to FATF members, non-members, observers, financial and other affected sectors and interested parties. This consultation process pro-

---

[1] The FATF is an inter-governmental body which sets standards, and develops and promotes policies to combat money laundering and terrorist financing. It currently has 33 members: 31 countries and governments and 2 international organisations; and more than 20 observers: 5 FATF-style regional bodies and more than 15 other international organisations or bodies. *A list of all members and observers* can be found at its website – *www.fatf-gafi.org*

vided a wide range of input, all of which was considered in the review process.

The revised Forty Recommendations now apply not only to money laundering but also to terrorist financing, and when combined with the Eight Special Recommendations on Terrorist Financing provide an enhanced, comprehensive and consistent framework of measures for combating money laundering and terrorist financing. The FATF recognises that countries have diverse legal and financial systems and so all cannot take identical measures to achieve the common objective, especially over matters of detail. The Recommendations therefore set minimum standards for action for countries to implement the detail according to their particular circumstances and constitutional frameworks. The Recommendations cover all the measures that national systems should have in place within their criminal justice and regulatory systems; the preventive measures to be taken by *financial institutions* and certain other businesses and professions; and international co-operation.

The original FATF Forty Recommendations were drawn up in 1990 as an initiative to combat the misuse of financial systems by persons laundering drug money. In 1996 the Recommendations were revised for the first time to reflect evolving money laundering typologies. The 1996 Forty Recommendations have been endorsed by more than 130 countries and are the international anti-money laundering standard.

In October 2001 the FATF expanded its mandate to deal

with the issue of the financing of terrorism, and took the important step of creating the Eight Special Recommendations on Terrorist Financing. These Recommendations contain a set of measures aimed at combating the funding of terrorist acts and terrorist organisations, and are complementary to the Forty Recommendations.[2]

A key element in the fight against money laundering and the financing of terrorism is the need for countries systems to be monitored and evaluated, with respect to these international standards. The mutual evaluations conducted by the FATF and FATF-style regional bodies, as well as the assessments conducted by the IMF and World Bank, are a vital mechanism for ensuring that the FATF Recommendations are effectively implemented by all countries.

LEGAL SYSTEMS
Scope of the criminal offence of money laundering

Recommendation 1

Countries should criminalise money laundering on the basis of United Nations Convention against Illicit Traffic in Narcotic Drugs and Psychotropic Substances, 1988 (the Vienna Convention) and United Nations Conven-

---

[2] The FATF Forty and Eight Special Recommendations have been recognised by the International Monetary Fund and the World Bank as the international standards for combating money laundering and the financing of terrorism.

tion against Transnational Organized Crime, 2000 (the Palermo Convention).

Countries should apply the crime of money laundering to all serious offences, with a view to including the widest range of predicate offences. Predicate offences may be described by reference to all offences, or to a threshold linked either to a category of serious offences or to the penalty of imprisonment applicable to the predicate offence (threshold approach), or to a list of predicate offences, or a combination of these approaches.

Where countries apply a threshold approach, predicate offences should at a minimum comprise all offences that fall within the category of serious offences under their national law or should include offences which are punishable by a maximum penalty of more than one year's imprisonment or for those countries that have a minimum threshold for offences in their legal system, predicate offences should comprise all offences, which are punished by a minimum penalty of more than six months imprisonment.

Whichever approach is adopted, each country should at a minimum include a range of offences within each of the designated categories of offences.[3]

Predicate offences for money laundering should extend to conduct that occurred in another country, which constitutes an offence in that country, and which would have

---

[3] See the definition of 'Designated categories of offences' available in the full document at *www.fatf-gafi.org*

constituted a predicate offence had it occurred domestically. Countries may provide that the only prerequisite is
that the conduct would have constituted a predicate
offence had it occurred domestically.

Countries may provide that the offence of money
laundering does not apply to persons who committed
the predicate offence, where this is required by fundamental principles of their domestic law.

Recommendation 2

Countries should ensure that:

(a) The intent and knowledge required to prove the
    offence of money laundering is consistent with the
    standards set forth in the Vienna and Palermo Con-
    ventions, including the concept that such mental state
    may be inferred from objective factual circumstances.
(b) Criminal liability, and, where that is not possible,
    civil or administrative liability, should apply to
    legal persons. This should not preclude parallel crim-
    inal, civil or administrative proceedings with respect
    to legal persons in countries in which such forms of
    liability are available. Legal persons should be subject
    to effective, proportionate and dissuasive sanctions.
    Such measures should be without prejudice to the
    criminal liability of individuals.

Provisional measures and confiscation

Recommendation 3

Countries should adopt measures similar to those set forth in the Vienna and Palermo Conventions, including legislative measures, to enable their competent authorities to confiscate property laundered, proceeds from money laundering or predicate offences, instrumentalities used in or intended for use in the commission of these offences, or property of corresponding value, without prejudicing the rights of bona fide third parties.

Such measures should include the authority to: (a) identify, trace and evaluate property which is subject to confiscation; (b) carry out provisional measures, such as freezing and seizing, to prevent any dealing, transfer or disposal of such property; (c) take steps that will prevent or void actions that prejudice the State's ability to recover property that is subject to confiscation; and (d) take any appropriate investigative measures.

Countries may consider adopting measures that allow such proceeds or instrumentalities to be confiscated without requiring a criminal conviction, or which require an offender to demonstrate the lawful origin of the property alleged to be liable to confiscation, to the extent that such a requirement is consistent with the principles of their domestic law.

MEASURES TO BE TAKEN BY FINANCIAL INSTITUTIONS AND NON-FINANCIAL BUSINESSES AND PROFESSIONS TO PREVENT MONEY LAUNDERING AND TERRORIST FINANCING

Recommendation 4

Countries should ensure that financial institution secrecy laws do not inhibit implementation of the FATF Recommendations.

Customer due diligence and record-keeping

Recommendation 5

Financial institutions should not keep anonymous accounts or accounts in obviously fictitious names.

Financial institutions should undertake customer due diligence measures, including identifying and verifying the identity of their customers, when:

- establishing business relations;
- carrying out occasional transactions: (i) above the applicable designated threshold; or (ii) that are wire transfers in the circumstances covered by the Interpretative Note to Special Recommendation VII (visit *www.fatf-gafi.org*);

- there is a suspicion of money laundering or terrorist financing; or
- the financial institution has doubts about the veracity or adequacy of previously obtained customer identification data.

The customer due diligence (*CDD*) measures to be taken are as follows:

(a) Identifying the customer and verifying that customer's identity using reliable, independent source documents, data or information.[4]
(b) Identifying the beneficial owner, and taking reasonable measures to verify the identity of the beneficial owner such that the financial institution is satisfied that it knows who the beneficial owner is. For legal persons and arrangements this should include financial institutions taking reasonable measures to understand the ownership and control structure of the customer.
(c) Obtaining information on the purpose and intended nature of the business relationship.
(d) Conducting ongoing due diligence on the business relationship and scrutiny of transactions undertaken throughout the course of that relationship to ensure that the transactions being conducted are consistent with the institution's knowledge of the customer, their business and risk profile, including, where necessary, the source of funds.

---

[4] Reliable, independent source documents, data or information will hereafter be referred to as 'identification data'.

Financial institutions should apply each of the CDD measures under (a) to (d) above, but may determine the extent of such measures on a risk sensitive basis depending on the type of customer, business relationship or transaction. The measures that are taken should be consistent with any guidelines issued by competent authorities. For higher risk categories, financial institutions should perform enhanced due diligence. In certain circumstances, where there are low risks, countries may decide that financial institutions can apply reduced or simplified measures.

Financial institutions should verify the identity of the customer and beneficial owner before or during the course of establishing a business relationship or conducting transactions for occasional customers. Countries may permit financial institutions to complete the verification as soon as reasonably practicable following the establishment of the relationship, where the money laundering risks are effectively managed and where this is essential not to interrupt the normal conduct of business.

Where the financial institution is unable to comply with paragraphs (a) to (c) above, it should not open the account, commence business relations or perform the transaction; or should terminate the business relationship; and should consider making a suspicious transactions report in relation to the customer.

These requirements should apply to all new customers, though financial institutions should also apply this Recommendation to existing customers on the basis of materiality and risk, and should conduct due diligence on such existing relationships at appropriate times. (See Interpretative Notes:[5] Recommendation 5 and Recommendations 5, 12 and 16.)

Recommendation 6

Financial institutions should, in relation to politically exposed persons, in addition to performing normal due diligence measures:

(a) Have appropriate risk management systems to determine whether the customer is a politically exposed person.

(b) Obtain senior management approval for establishing business relationships with such customers.

(c) Take reasonable measures to establish the source of wealth and source of funds.

(d) Conduct enhanced ongoing monitoring of the business relationship. (See Interpretative Note.[5])

Recommendation 7

Financial institutions should, in relation to cross-border correspondent banking and other similar relationships, in addition to performing normal due diligence measures:

(a) Gather sufficient information about a respondent institution to understand fully the nature of the respondent's business and to determine from publicly available information the reputation of the institution

---

[5] The Interpretative Notes can be found in the full document, available at *www.fatf-gafi.org*

and the quality of supervision, including whether it has been subject to a money laundering or terrorist financing investigation or regulatory action.

(b) Assess the respondent institution's anti-money laundering and terrorist financing controls.

(c) Obtain approval from senior management before establishing new correspondent relationships.

(d) Document the respective responsibilities of each institution.

(e) With respect to 'payable-through accounts', be satisfied that the respondent bank has verified the identity of and performed on-going due diligence on the customers having direct access to accounts of the correspondent and that it is able to provide relevant customer identification data upon request to the correspondent bank.

Recommendation 8

Financial institutions should pay special attention to any money laundering threats that may arise from new or developing technologies that might favour anonymity, and take measures, if needed, to prevent their use in money laundering schemes. In particular, financial institutions should have policies and procedures in place to address any specific risks associated with non-face to face business relationships or transactions.

Recommendation 9

Countries may permit financial institutions to rely on intermediaries or other third parties to perform elements (a)–(c) of the CDD process or to introduce business, provided that the criteria set out below are met. Where such reliance is permitted, the ultimate responsibility for customer identification and verification remains with the financial institution relying on the third party.

The criteria that should be met are as follows:

(a) A financial institution relying upon a third party should immediately obtain the necessary information concerning elements (a)–(c) of the CDD process. Financial institutions should take adequate steps to satisfy themselves that copies of identification data and other relevant documentation relating to the CDD requirements will be made available from the third party upon request without delay.

(b) The financial institution should satisfy itself that the third party is regulated and supervised for, and has measures in place to comply with CDD requirements in line with Recommendations 5 and 10.

It is left to each country to determine in which countries the third party that meets the conditions can be based, having regard to information available on countries that do not or do not adequately apply the FATF Recommendations. (See Interpretative Note at *www.fatf-gafi.org*)

Recommendation 10

Financial institutions should maintain, for at least five years, all necessary records on transactions, both domestic or international, to enable them to comply swiftly with information requests from the competent authorities. Such records must be sufficient to permit reconstruction of individual transactions (including the amounts and types of currency involved if any) so as to provide, if necessary, evidence for prosecution of criminal activity.

Financial institutions should keep records on the identification data obtained through the customer due diligence process (e.g., copies or records of official identification documents like passports, identity cards, driving licenses or similar documents), account files and business correspondence for at least five years after the business relationship is ended.

The identification data and transaction records should be available to domestic competent authorities upon appropriate authority. (See Interpretative Notes at *www.fatf-gafi.org*)

Recommendation 11

Financial institutions should pay special attention to all complex, unusual large transactions, and all unusual patterns of transactions, which have no apparent economic or visible lawful purpose. The background and purpose of such transactions should, as far as possible, be examined, the findings established in writing, and be available to help competent authorities and auditors. (See Interpretative Notes at *www.fatf-gafi.org*)

Recommendation 12

The customer due diligence and record-keeping requirements set out in Recommendations 5, 6, and 8 to 11 apply to designated non-financial businesses and professions in the following situations:

(a) Casinos – when customers engage in financial trans-actions equal to or above the applicable designated threshold.

(b) Real estate agents - when they are involved in transac-tions for their client concerning the buying and selling of real estate.

(c) Dealers in precious metals and dealers in precious stones - when they engage in any cash transaction with a customer equal to or above the applicable designated threshold.

(d) Lawyers, notaries, other independent legal profes-sionals and accountants when they prepare for or carry out transactions for their client concerning the following activities:
   ○ buying and selling of real estate;
   ○ managing of client money, securities or other assets;
   ○ management of bank, savings or securities accounts;
   ○ organisation of contributions for the creation, operation or management of companies;
   ○ creation, operation or management of legal persons or arrangements, and buying and selling of busi-ness entities.

(e) Trust and company service providers when they prepare for or carry out transactions for a client con-cerning the activities listed in the definition in the FATF Glossary. (See Interpretative Notes and Glos-sary at *www.fatf-gafi.org*)

Reporting of suspicious transactions and compliance

Recommendation 13

If a financial institution suspects or has reasonable grounds to suspect that funds are the proceeds of a criminal activity, or are related to terrorist financing, it should be required, directly by law or regulation, to report promptly its suspicions to the financial intelligence unit (*FIU*). (See Interpretative Notes at *www.fatf-gafi.org*)

Recommendation 14

Financial institutions, their directors, officers and employees should be:

(a) Protected by legal provisions from criminal and civil liability for breach of any restriction on disclosure of information imposed by contract or by any legislative, regulatory or administrative provision, if they report their suspicions in good faith to the FIU, even if they did not know precisely what the underlying criminal activity was, and regardless of whether illegal activity actually occurred.

(b) Prohibited by law from disclosing the fact that a suspicious transaction report (STR) or related information is being reported to the FIU. (See Interpretative Notes at *www.fatf-gafi.org*)

Recommendation 15

Financial institutions should develop programmes against money laundering and terrorist financing. These programmes should include:

(a) The development of internal policies, procedures and controls, including appropriate compliance management arrangements, and adequate screening procedures to ensure high standards when hiring employees.
(b) An ongoing employee training programme.
(c) An audit function to test the system. (See Interpretative Notes at *www.fatf-gafi.org*)

Recommendation 16

The requirements set out in Recommendations 13 to 15, and 21 apply to all designated non-financial businesses and professions, subject to the following qualifications:

(a) Lawyers, notaries, other independent legal professionals and accountants should be required to report suspicious transactions when, on behalf of or for a client, they engage in a financial transaction in relation to the activities described in Recommendation 12(d). Countries are strongly encouraged to extend the reporting requirement to the rest of the professional activities of accountants, including auditing.
(b) Dealers in precious metals and dealers in precious stones should be required to report suspicious transactions when they engage in any cash transaction with a

customer equal to or above the applicable designated threshold.

(c) Trust and company service providers should be required to report suspicious transactions for a client when, on behalf of or for a client, they engage in a transaction in relation to the activities referred to Recommendation 12(e).

Lawyers, notaries, other independent legal professionals, and accountants acting as independent legal professionals, are not required to report their suspicions if the relevant information was obtained in circumstances where they are subject to professional secrecy or legal professional privilege. (See Interpretative Notes at *www.fatf-gafi.org*: Recommendation 16 and Recommendations 5, 12, and 16.)

Other measures to deter money laundering and terrorist financing

Recommendation 17

Countries should ensure that effective, proportionate and dissuasive sanctions, whether criminal, civil or administrative, are available to deal with natural or legal persons covered by these Recommendations that fail to comply with anti-money laundering or terrorist financing requirements.

Recommendation 18

Countries should not approve the establishment or accept the continued operation of shell banks. Financial institutions should refuse to enter into, or continue, a correspondent banking relationship with shell banks. Financial institutions should also guard against establishing relations with respondent foreign financial institutions that permit their accounts to be used by shell banks.

Recommendation 19

Countries should consider the feasibility and utility of a system where banks and other financial institutions and intermediaries would report all domestic and international currency transactions above a fixed amount, to a national central agency with a computerised data base, available to competent authorities for use in money laundering or terrorist financing cases, subject to strict safeguards to ensure proper use of the information. (Modified 22 October 2004.)

Recommendation 20

Countries should consider applying the FATF Recommendations to businesses and professions, other than designated non-financial businesses and professions, that pose a money laundering or terrorist financing risk.

Countries should further encourage the development of modern and secure techniques of money management that are less vulnerable to money laundering.

Measures to be taken with respect to countries that do not or insufficiently comply with the FATF Recommendations

Recommendation 21

Financial institutions should give special attention to business relationships and transactions with persons, including companies and financial institutions, from countries which do not or insufficiently apply the FATF Recommendations. Whenever these transactions have no apparent economic or visible lawful purpose, their background and purpose should, as far as possible, be examined, the findings established in writing, and be available to help competent authorities. Where such a country continues not to apply or insufficiently applies the FATF Recommendations, countries should be able to apply appropriate countermeasures.

Recommendation 22

Financial institutions should ensure that the principles applicable to financial institutions, which are mentioned above are also applied to branches and majority owned subsidiaries located abroad, especially in countries which do not or insufficiently apply the FATF Recommendations, to the extent that local applicable laws and regulations permit. When local applicable laws and regulations prohibit this implementation, competent authorities in the country of the parent institution should be informed by the financial institutions that they cannot apply the FATF Recommendations.

Regulation and supervision

Recommendation 23

Countries should ensure that financial institutions are subject to adequate regulation and supervision and are effectively implementing the FATF Recommendations. Competent authorities should take the necessary legal or regulatory measures to prevent criminals or their associates from holding or being the beneficial owner of a significant or controlling interest or holding a management function in a financial institution.

For financial institutions subject to the Core Principles, the regulatory and supervisory measures that apply for prudential purposes and which are also relevant to money laundering, should apply in a similar manner for anti-money laundering and terrorist financing purposes.

Other financial institutions should be licensed or registered and appropriately regulated, and subject to supervision or oversight for anti-money laundering purposes, having regard to the risk of money laundering or terrorist financing in that sector. At a minimum, businesses providing a service of money or value transfer, or of money or currency changing should be licensed or registered, and subject to effective systems for monitoring and ensuring compliance with national requirements to combat money laundering and terrorist financing. (See Interpretative Notes at *www.fatf-gafi.org*)

Recommendation 24

Designated non-financial businesses and professions should be subject to regulatory and supervisory measures as set out below.

(a) Casinos should be subject to a comprehensive regulatory and supervisory regime that ensures that they have effectively implemented the necessary anti-money laundering and terrorist-financing measures. At a minimum:
  o casinos should be licensed;
  o competent authorities should take the necessary legal or regulatory measures to prevent criminals or their associates from holding or being the beneficial owner of a significant or controlling interest, holding a management function in, or being an operator of a casino;
  o competent authorities should ensure that casinos are effectively supervised for compliance with requirements to combat money laundering and terrorist financing.

(b) Countries should ensure that the other categories of designated non-financial businesses and professions are subject to effective systems for monitoring and ensuring their compliance with requirements to combat money laundering and terrorist financing. This should be performed on a risk-sensitive basis. This may be performed by a government authority or by an appropriate self-regulatory organisation, provided that such an organisation can ensure that its members comply with their obligations to combat money laundering and terrorist financing.

Recommendation 25

The competent authorities should establish guidelines, and provide feedback which will assist financial institutions and designated non-financial businesses and professions in applying national measures to combat money laundering and terrorist financing, and in particular, in detecting and reporting suspicious transactions. (See Interpretative Notes at *www.fatf-gafi.org*)

INSTITUTIONAL AND OTHER MEASURES NECESSARY IN SYSTEMS FOR COMBATING MONEY LAUNDERING AND TERRORIST FINANCING

Competent authorities, their powers and resources

Recommendation 26

Countries should establish a FIU that serves as a national centre for the receiving (and, as permitted, requesting), analysis and dissemination of STR and other information regarding potential money laundering or terrorist financing. The FIU should have access, directly or indirectly, on a timely basis to the financial, administrative and law enforcement information that it requires to properly undertake its functions, including the analysis of STR. (See Interpretative Notes at *www.fatf-gafi.org*)

Recommendation 27

Countries should ensure that designated law enforcement authorities have responsibility for money laundering and terrorist financing investigations. Countries are encouraged to support and develop, as far as possible, special investigative techniques suitable for the investigation of money laundering, such as controlled delivery, undercover operations and other relevant techniques. Countries are also encouraged to use other effective mechanisms such as the use of permanent or temporary groups specialised in asset investigation, and co-operative investigations with appropriate competent authorities in other countries. (See Interpretative Notes at *www.fatf-gafi.org*)

Recommendation 28

When conducting investigations of money laundering and underlying predicate offences, competent authorities should be able to obtain documents and information for use in those investigations, and in prosecutions and related actions. This should include powers to use compulsory measures for the production of records held by financial institutions and other persons, for the search of persons and premises, and for the seizure and obtaining of evidence.

Recommendation 29

Supervisors should have adequate powers to monitor and ensure compliance by financial institutions with requirements to combat money laundering and terrorist financing, including the authority to conduct inspections. They should be authorised to compel production of any information from financial institutions that is relevant to monitoring such compliance, and to impose adequate administrative sanctions for failure to comply with such requirements.

Recommendation 30

Countries should provide their competent authorities involved in combating money laundering and terrorist financing with adequate financial, human and technical resources. Countries should have in place processes to ensure that the staff of those authorities are of high integrity.

Recommendation 31

Countries should ensure that policy makers, the FIU, law enforcement and supervisors have effective mechanisms in place which enable them to co-operate, and where appropriate co-ordinate domestically with each other concerning the development and implementation of policies and activities to combat money laundering and terrorist financing.

Recommendation 32

Countries should ensure that their competent authorities can review the effectiveness of their systems to combat money laundering and terrorist financing systems by maintaining comprehensive statistics on matters relevant to the effectiveness and efficiency of such systems. This should include statistics on the STR received and disseminated; on money laundering and terrorist financing investigations, prosecutions and convictions; on property frozen, seized and confiscated; and on mutual legal assistance or other international requests for co-operation.

Transparency of legal persons and arrangements

Recommendation 33

Countries should take measures to prevent the unlawful use of legal persons by money launderers. Countries should ensure that there is adequate, accurate and timely information on the beneficial ownership and control of legal persons that can be obtained or accessed in a timely fashion by competent authorities. In particular, countries that have legal persons that are able to issue bearer shares should take appropriate measures to ensure that they are not misused for money laundering and be able to demonstrate the adequacy of those measures. Countries could consider measures to facilitate access to beneficial ownership and control information to financial institutions undertaking the requirements set out in Recommendation 5.

Recommendation 34

Countries should take measures to prevent the unlawful use of legal arrangements by money launderers. In particular, countries should ensure that there is adequate, accurate and timely information on express trusts, including information on the settlor, trustee and beneficiaries, that can be obtained or accessed in a timely fashion by competent authorities. Countries could consider measures to facilitate access to beneficial ownership and control information to financial institutions undertaking the requirements set out in Recommendation 5.

INTERNATIONAL CO-OPERATION

Recommendation 35

Countries should take immediate steps to become party to and implement fully the Vienna Convention, the Palermo Convention, and the 1999 United Nations International Convention for the Suppression of the Financing of Terrorism. Countries are also encouraged to ratify and implement other relevant international conventions, such as the 1990 Council of Europe Convention on Laundering, Search, Seizure and Confiscation of the Proceeds from Crime and the 2002 Inter-American Convention against Terrorism.

Mutual legal assistance and extradition

Recommendation 36

Countries should rapidly, constructively and effectively provide the widest possible range of mutual legal assistance in relation to money laundering and terrorist financing investigations, prosecutions, and related proceedings. In particular, countries should:

(a) Not prohibit or place unreasonable or unduly restrictive conditions on the provision of mutual legal assistance.

(b) Ensure that they have clear and efficient processes for the execution of mutual legal assistance requests.

(c) Not refuse to execute a request for mutual legal assistance on the sole ground that the offence is also considered to involve fiscal matters.

(d) Not refuse to execute a request for mutual legal assistance on the grounds that laws require financial institutions to maintain secrecy or confidentiality.

Countries should ensure that the powers of their competent authorities required under Recommendation 28 are also available for use in response to requests for mutual legal assistance, and if consistent with their domestic framework, in response to direct requests from foreign judicial or law enforcement authorities to domestic counterparts.

To avoid conflicts of jurisdiction, consideration should be given to devising and applying mechanisms for determining the best venue for prosecution of defendants in the interests of justice in cases that are subject to prosecution in more than one country.

Recommendation 37

Countries should, to the greatest extent possible, render mutual legal assistance notwithstanding the absence of dual criminality.

Where dual criminality is required for mutual legal assistance or extradition, that requirement should be deemed to be satisfied regardless of whether both countries place the offence within the same category of offence or denominate the offence by the same terminology, provided that both countries criminalise the conduct underlying the offence.

Recommendation 38

There should be authority to take expeditious action in response to requests by foreign countries to identify, freeze, seize and confiscate property laundered, proceeds from money laundering or predicate offences, instrumentalities used in or intended for use in the commission of these offences, or property of corresponding value. There should also be arrangements for co-ordinating seizure and confiscation proceedings, which may include the sharing of confiscated assets. (See Interpretative Notes at *www.fatf-gafi.org*)

Recommendation 39

Countries should recognise money laundering as an extraditable offence. Each country should either extradite its own nationals, or where a country does not do so solely on the grounds of nationality, that country should, at the request of the country seeking extradition, submit the case without undue delay to its competent authorities for the purpose of prosecution of the offences set forth in the request. Those authorities should take their decision and conduct their proceedings in the same manner as in the case of any other offence of a serious nature under the domestic law of that country. The countries concerned should cooperate with each other, in particular on procedural and evidentiary aspects, to ensure the efficiency of such prosecutions. Subject to their legal frameworks, countries may consider simplifying extradition by allowing direct transmission of extradition requests between appropriate ministries, extraditing persons based only on warrants of arrests or judgements, and/or introducing a simplified extradition of consenting persons who waive formal extradition proceedings.

Other forms of co-operation

Recommendation 40

Countries should ensure that their competent authorities provide the widest possible range of international co-operation to their foreign counterparts. There should be clear and effective gateways to facilitate the prompt and constructive exchange directly between counterparts, either spontaneously or upon request, of information relating to both money laundering and the underlying predicate offences. Exchanges should be permitted without unduly restrictive conditions. In particular:

(a) Competent authorities should not refuse a request for assistance on the sole ground that the request is also considered to involve fiscal matters.

(b) Countries should not invoke laws that require financial institutions to maintain secrecy or confidentiality as a ground for refusing to provide co-operation.

(c) Competent authorities should be able to conduct inquiries; and where possible, investigations; on behalf of foreign counterparts.

Where the ability to obtain information sought by a foreign competent authority is not within the mandate of its counterpart, countries are also encouraged to permit a prompt and constructive exchange of information with non-counterparts. Co-operation with foreign authorities other than counterparts could occur directly or indirectly. When uncertain about the appropriate avenue to follow, competent authorities should first contact their foreign counterparts for assistance.

Countries should establish controls and safeguards to ensure that information exchanged by competent authorities is used only in an authorised manner, consistent with their obligations concerning privacy and data protection.

NINE SPECIAL RECOMMENDATIONS ON TERRORIST FINANCING

Recognising the vital importance of taking action to combat the financing of terrorism, the FATF has agreed these Recommendations, which, when combined with the FATF Forty Recommendations on money laundering, set out the basic framework to detect, prevent and suppress the financing of terrorism and terrorist acts.

I Ratification and implementation of UN instruments

Each country should take immediate steps to ratify and to implement fully the 1999 United Nations International Convention for the Suppression of the Financing of Terrorism. Countries should also immediately implement the United Nations resolutions relating to the prevention and suppression of the financing of terrorist acts, particularly United Nations Security Council Resolution 1373.

II Criminalising the financing of terrorism and associated money laundering

Each country should criminalise the financing of terrorism, terrorist acts and terrorist organisations. Countries should ensure that such offences are designated as money laundering predicate offences.

III Freezing and confiscating terrorist assets

Each country should implement measures to freeze without delay funds or other assets of terrorists, those who finance terrorism and terrorist organisations in accordance with the United Nations resolutions relating to the prevention and suppression of the financing of terrorist acts.

Each country should also adopt and implement measures, including legislative ones, which would enable the competent authorities to seize and confiscate property that is the proceeds of, or used in, or intended or allocated for use in, the financing of terrorism, terrorist acts or terrorist organisations.

IV Reporting suspicious transactions related to terrorism

If financial institutions, or other businesses or entities subject to anti-money laundering obligations, suspect or have reasonable grounds to suspect that funds are linked or related to, or are to be used for terrorism, terrorist acts or by terrorist organisations, they should be required to report promptly their suspicions to the competent authorities.

V International co-operation

Each country should afford another country, on the basis of a treaty, arrangement or other mechanism for mutual legal assistance or information exchange, the greatest possible measure of assistance in connection with criminal, civil enforcement, and administrative investigations, inquiries and proceedings relating to the financing of terrorism, terrorist acts and terrorist organisations.

Countries should also take all possible measures to ensure that they do not provide safe havens for individuals charged with the financing of terrorism, terrorist acts or terrorist organisations, and should have procedures in place to extradite, where possible, such individuals.

VI   Alternative remittance

Each country should take measures to ensure that persons or legal entities, including agents, that provide a service for the transmission of money or value, including transmission through an informal money or value transfer system or network, should be licensed or registered and subject to all the FATF Recommendations that apply to banks and non-bank financial institutions. Each country should ensure that persons or legal entities that carry out this service illegally are subject to administrative, civil or criminal sanctions.

VII   Wire transfers

Countries should take measures to require financial institutions, including money remitters, to include accurate and meaningful originator information (name, address and account number) on funds transfers and related messages that are sent, and the information should remain with the transfer or related message through the payment chain.

Countries should take measures to ensure that financial

institutions, including money remitters, conduct en-hanced scrutiny of and monitor for suspicious activity funds transfers which do not contain complete originator information (name, address and account number).

VIII   Non-profit organisations

Countries should review the adequacy of laws and reg-ulations that relate to entities that can be abused for the financing of terrorism. Non-profit organisations are par-ticularly vulnerable, and countries should ensure that they cannot be misused:

- by terrorist organisations posing as legitimate entities;
- to exploit legitimate entities as conduits for terrorist financing, including for the purpose of escaping asset freezing measures; and
- to conceal or obscure the clandestine diversion of funds intended for legitimate purposes to terrorist organisations.

IX   Cash couriers

Countries should have measures in place to detect the physical cross-border transportation of currency and bearer negotiable instruments, including a declaration system or other disclosure obligation.

Countries should ensure that their competent authorities have the legal authority to stop or restrain currency or bearer negotiable instruments that are suspected to be related to terrorist financing or money laundering, or that are falsely declared or disclosed.

Countries should ensure that effective, proportionate and dissuasive sanctions are available to deal with persons who make false declaration(s) or disclosure(s). In cases where the currency or bearer negotiable instruments are related to terrorist financing or money laundering, countries should also adopt measures, including legislative ones consistent with Recommendation 3 and Special Recommendation III, which would enable the confiscation of such currency or instruments.

NOTE:

With the adoption of Special Recommendation IX, the FATF now deletes paragraph 19(a) of Recommendation 19 and the Interpretative Note (see *www.fatf-gafi.org*) to Recommendation 19 in order to ensure internal consistency amongst the FATF Recommendations. The modified text of recommendation 19 reads as follows:

Recommendation 19

Countries should consider the feasibility and utility of a system where banks and other financial institutions and intermediaries would report all domestic and international currency transactions above a fixed amount, to a national central agency with a computerised data base, available to competent authorities for use in money laundering or terrorist financing cases, subject to strict safeguards to ensure proper use of the information.

Appendix

B

....

FATF–GAFI

Financial Action Task Force (*FATF*) will explore the symbiotic relationship among corruption, money laundering and terrorist financing.

Over 400 delegates from 32 jurisdictions and 16 international organisations attended the FATF Plenary meeting held in Paris on 12–14 October 2004. Professor Kader Asmal, of the Republic of South Africa, assumed the chairmanship of the FATF. He noted that his country is one of the newest members of the organisation, having joined the FATF in June 2003. 'I am proud to lead this organisation. This demonstrates the strong commitment of African countries to take a role in combating the scourges of international crime.'

At this meeting, the FATF also launched an ambitious project, in partnership with the Asia/Pacific Group on Money Laundering to explore the symbiotic relationship among corruption, money laundering and terrorist financing and how the FATF's AML/CFT experience can best be used to combat these combined threats.

The FATF also welcomed the UN Security Council Resolution 1617 (2005), which 'strongly urges all Member States to implement the comprehensive, international standards' embodied in the FATF 40 Recommendations on money laundering and the Nine Special Recommendations on terrorist financing. The formal endorsement of the FATF standards by the UN Security Council is a major step toward effective implementation of the Recommendations throughout the world.

At this meeting, the FATF reviewed the anti-money

laundering and counter-terrorist financing systems of three countries: Australia, Italy and Switzerland. Preliminary outcomes of the third round of mutual evaluations show that while FATF members are making very serious efforts to implement the new standards, effective implementation will take further effort. Therefore, the FATF will continue to closely monitor the progress of all its members.

'We must continue to strengthen partnerships around the world if we are to win this war against money laundering and terrorist financing' Professor Asmal said. To achieve that goal, the FATF decided to further enhance its partnerships with regional bodies to improve the effectiveness of the global network against money laundering and terrorist financing. In this spirit, the FATF will invite the members of the Eastern and Southern Africa Anti-Money Laundering Group (*ESAAMLG*) to participate in a joint session with the FATF at its next Plenary meeting to be held in February 2006 in Cape Town. South Africa is a member of both organisations.

FATF members will also join with members of GAFISUD, the South American regional body, in November to study emerging threats in the areas of new payment technologies, the use of corporate vehicles and trade-based money laundering.

The FATF removed Nauru from its list of non-cooperative countries and territories (*NCCTs*) after Nauru abolished its 400 shell banks, thus removing the major money laundering risk. Though Myanmar and Nigeria remain on the list of NCCTs, the FATF recognised that they have adopted many necessary legal reforms and encouraged further implementation. In the meantime, the FATF continues to call on financial institutions to scrutinise transactions with persons, businesses or banks in these countries, as per Recommendation 21.

Appendix

C

. . . .

CONSOLIDATED KYC RISK MANAGEMENT

Source: Basel Committee on Banking Supervision, Bank for International Settlements

INTRODUCTION

1. The adoption of effective know your customer (*KYC*) standards is an essential part of banks' risk management practices. Banks with inadequate KYC risk management programmes may be subject to significant risks, especially legal and reputational risk. Sound KYC policies and procedures not only contribute to a bank's overall safety and soundness, they also protect the integrity of the banking system by reducing the likelihood of banks becoming vehicles for money laundering, terrorist financing and other unlawful activities. Recent initiatives to reinforce actions against terrorism in particular have underlined the importance of banks' ability to monitor their customers wherever they conduct business.

2. In October 2001, the Basel Committee on Banking Supervision (*BCBS*) issued *Customer Due Diligence for Banks*,[1] subsequently reinforced by a *General Guide to Account Opening and Customer Identification* (*CDD*) in February 2003. The CDD paper outlines four essential elements necessary for a sound KYC programme. These elements are: (i) customer acceptance policy; (ii) customer identification; (iii) ongoing monitoring of higher risk accounts; and (iv) risk management. The principles laid down have been accepted and widely adopted by jurisdictions throughout the world as a benchmark for commercial banks and a good practice guideline for other categories of financial institution.

---

[1] Basel Committe on Banking Supervision, October 2001.

3. A key challenge in implementing sound KYC policies and procedures is how to put in place an effective group-wide approach. The legal and reputational risks identified in paragraph 1 are global in nature. As such, it is essential that each group develop a global risk management programme supported by policies that incorporate group-wide KYC standards. Policies and procedures at the branch- or subsidiary-level must be consistent with and supportive of the group KYC standards even where for local or business reasons such policies and procedures are not identical to the group's.[2]

4. Consolidated KYC Risk Management means an established centralised process for coordinating and promulgating policies and procedures on a groupwide basis, as well as robust arrangements for the sharing of information within the group. Policies and procedures should be designed not merely to comply strictly with all relevant laws and regulations, but more broadly to identify, monitor and mitigate reputational, operational, legal and concentration risks. Similar to the approach to consolidated credit, market and operational risk, effective control of consolidated KYC risk requires banks to coordinate their risk management activities on a groupwide basis across the head office and all branches and subsidiaries.

---

[2] The term 'group' is used in this paper to refer to an organisation's one or more banks, and the branches and subsidiaries of those banks. The term 'head office' is used in this paper to refer also to the parent bank or to the unit in which KYC risk management is performed on a business line basis.

5. The BCBS recognises that implementing effective KYC procedures on a groupwide basis is more challenging than many other risk management processes because KYC involves in most cases the liabilities rather than the assets side of the balance sheet, as well as balances that are carried as off-balance sheet items. For reasons of customer privacy, some jurisdictions continue to restrict banks' ability to transmit names and balances as regards customer liabilities whereas there are now very few countries maintaining similar barriers on the assets side of the balance sheet. It is essential, in conducting effective monitoring on a groupwide basis, that banks be free to pass information about their liabilities or assets under management, subject to adequate legal protection, back to their head offices or parent bank. This applies in the case of both branches and subsidiaries. The conditions under which this might be achieved are set out in paragraphs [20 to 23].

6. Jurisdictions should facilitate consolidated KYC risk management by providing an appropriate legal framework which allows the cross-border sharing of information. Legal restrictions that impede effective consolidated KYC risk management processes should be removed.

GLOBAL PROCESS FOR MANAGING KYC RISKS

7. The four essential elements of a sound KYC programme should be incorporated into a bank's risk man-

agement and control procedures to ensure that all aspects of KYC risk are identified and can be appropriately mitigated. Hence, a bank should aim to apply the same risk management, customer acceptance policy, procedures for customer identification, and process for monitoring its accounts throughout its branches and subsidiaries around the world. Every effort should be made to ensure that the group's ability to obtain and review information in accordance with its global KYC standards is not impaired as a result of modifications to local policies or procedures necessitated by local legal requirements. In this regard banks should have robust information sharing between the head office and all branches and subsidiaries. Where the minimum KYC requirements of the home and host countries differ, offices in host jurisdictions should apply the higher standard of the two, subject to the direction given in CDD paragraph 66.

RISK MANAGEMENT

8. Groupwide KYC risk management programmes should include proper management oversight, systems and controls, segregation of duties, training and other related policies (CDD paragraph 55). The risk management programme should be implemented on a global basis. Explicit responsibility should be allocated within the bank for ensuring that the bank's policies and procedures for the risk management programme are managed effectively and are in accordance with the bank's global standards for customer identification,

ongoing monitoring of accounts and transactions, and the sharing of relevant information.

9. Banks' compliance and internal audit staffs, or external auditors, should evaluate adherence to all aspects of their group's standards for KYC, including the effectiveness of centralised KYC functions and the requirements for sharing information with other group members and responding to queries from head office. Internationally active banking groups need both an internal audit and a global compliance function since these are the principal and in some circumstances the only mechanisms for monitoring the application of the bank's global KYC standards and supporting policies and procedures, including the effectiveness of the procedures for sharing information within the group.

CUSTOMER ACCEPTANCE AND IDENTIFICATION POLICY

10. A bank should develop clear customer acceptance policies and procedures that include guidance on the types of customers that are likely to pose a higher than average risk to the bank (CDD paragraph 20), including managerial review of such prospective customers where appropriate.

11. Similarly, a bank should establish a risk-based systematic procedure for verifying the identity of new customers (CDD paragraph 22). It should develop standards on what records are to be obtained and retained for

customer identification on a global basis, including enhanced due diligence requirements for higher risk customers.

12. A bank should obtain appropriate identification information and maintain such information in a readily retrievable format so as to adequately identify its customers,[3] as well as fulfil any local reporting requirements. Relevant information should be accessible for purposes of information sharing among the banking group's head office, branches and subsidiaries. Each office of the banking group should be in a position to comply with minimum identification and accessibility standards applied by the head office.

13. These customer acceptance, customer identification and record-keeping standards should be implemented with consistent policies and procedures throughout the organisation, with adjustment as necessary to address variances in risk according to specific business line or geographic areas of operation. Moreover, it is recognised that different approaches to information collection and retention may be necessary across jurisdictions to conform with local regulatory requirements or relative risk factors.

---

[3] See customer identification requirements in the *General Guide to Account Opening and Customer Identification*, an attachment to the Basel Committee's Customer due diligence for banks (October 2001) paper – visit *www.bis.org*

MONITORING OF ACCOUNTS AND TRANSACTIONS

14. An essential element for addressing higher risks is the coordinated approach to the monitoring of customer account activity on a groupwide basis, regardless of whether the accounts are held on- or off-balance sheet, as assets under management or on a fiduciary basis (CDD paragraph 16). Banks should have standards for monitoring account activity for potentially suspicious transactions that are implemented by supporting policies and procedures throughout its branches and subsidiaries worldwide. They should be risk-based and emphasise the need to monitor material intra- and inter-country account activity.

15. Each office should maintain and monitor information on its accounts and transactions. This local monitoring should be complemented by a robust process of information sharing between the head office and its branches and subsidiaries regarding accounts and activity that may represent heightened risk.

16. In recent years, many banks have begun centralising certain processing systems and databases for internal risk management or efficiency purposes. In these circumstances, banks should complement local monitoring with transactions monitoring at the centralised site. This approach provides banks with the opportunity to monitor for patterns of suspicious activity that cannot be observed from the local site.

GROUPWIDE INFORMATION SHARING

17. Banks should centralise the responsibility for co-ordinating groupwide information sharing. Subsidiaries and branches should be required to proactively provide information concerning higher risk customers and activities relevant to the global management of reputational and legal risks to, and respond to requests for account information from the head office or parent bank in a timely manner. The bank's policies and procedures should include a description of the process to be followed for investigating and reporting potentially suspicious activity.

18. The bank's centralised KYC function should evaluate the potential risk posed by activity reported by its branches and subsidiaries and where appropriate assess its worldwide exposure to a given customer. The bank should have policies and procedures for ascertaining whether other branches or subsidiaries hold accounts for the same party and assessing the groupwide reputational, legal, concentration and operational risks. The bank should also have procedures governing global account relationships that are deemed potentially suspicious, detailing escalation procedures and guidance on restricting activities, including the closing of accounts as appropriate.

19. In addition, banks and their local offices should be responsive to requests from their respective law enforcement authorities for information about account holders

that is needed in the authorities' effort to combat money laundering and the financing of terrorism. Head office should be able to require all offices to search their files against a list of individuals or organisations suspected of aiding and abetting terrorist financing or money laundering, and report matches.

THE ROLE OF THE SUPERVISOR

20. Supervisors should verify that appropriate internal controls for KYC are in place and that banks are in compliance with supervisory and regulatory guidance. The supervisory process should include not only a review of policies and procedures but also a review of customer files and the sampling of accounts (CDD paragraph 61).

21. In a cross-border context, home country supervisors[4] should face no impediments in verifying a branch or subsidiary's compliance with groupwide KYC policies and procedures during on-site inspections. This may well require a review of customer files and a sampling of accounts. Home country supervisors should have access to information on sampled individual customer accounts to the extent necessary to enable a proper evaluation of the application of KYC standards and an assessment of risk management practices, and should not be impeded by local bank secrecy laws. In the case of branches or subsidiaries of international banking groups,

---

[4] In those countries where the examination process is undertaken by external auditors, this exemption should also apply to the competent auditors.

the host country supervisor retains responsibility for the supervision of compliance with local KYC regulations (which would include an evaluation of the appropriateness of the procedures).

22. The role of audit is particularly important in the evaluation of adherence to KYC standards on a consolidated basis and home country supervisors should ensure that appropriate frequency, resources and procedures are established in this regard and that they have full access to any relevant reports and working papers prepared through the audit process.

23. Safeguards are needed to ensure that information regarding individual accounts has the same confidentiality threshold afforded other information obtained through the supervisory process. A statement of mutual cooperation to facilitate information sharing between the two supervisors may well be helpful in this regard (CDD paragraph 68).

LEGAL IMPEDIMENTS

24. Although gateways are in place in most jurisdictions to enable banks to share information with their head offices for risk management purposes, some countries have rigorous bank secrecy or data protection laws that prevent, or can be interpreted as preventing, the transfer of such information. In such circumstances, banks overseas offices may be inclined to take a cautious stance regarding the transfer of customer information to their

head offices which may conflict with the consolidated KYC objective.

25. It is essential that all jurisdictions that host foreign banks provide an appropriate legal framework which allows information for KYC risk management purposes to be passed to the head office/parent bank and home country supervisors. Similarly, there should be no impediments to on-site visits by head office auditors, risk managers, compliance officers or home country supervisors, nor any restrictions on their ability to access all the local office's records, including customers names and balances. This access should be the same for both branches and subsidiaries. If impediments to information sharing prove to be insurmountable, and there are no satisfactory alternative arrangements, the home supervisor should make it clear to the host that the bank may decide for itself, or be required by its home supervisor, to close down the operation in question (CDD paragraph 69).

26. Where banks' head office staff are granted access to information on local customers, there should be no restrictions on them reporting such information back to head office. Such information should be subject to applicable privacy and privilege laws in the home country.

27. Subject to the conditions set out above, the BCBS believes that there is no justifiable reason why local legislation should impede the passage of customer information from a bank branch or subsidiary to its head office

or parent bank for risk management purposes. If the law restricts disclosure of information to third parties it is essential that the head office or parent bank is clearly excluded from the definition of a third party. Jurisdictions that have legislation that impedes, or can be interpreted as impeding, such information sharing are urged to remove any such restrictions and to provide specific gateways.

MIXED FINANCIAL GROUPS

28. Many banking groups now engage in securities and insurance businesses. Customer due diligence by mixed financial groups poses issues that may not be present for a pure banking group. Mixed groups should have systems and processes in place to monitor and share information on the identity of customers and account activity of the entire group, and to be alert to customers that use their services in different sectors. A customer relationship issue that arises in one part of a group would affect the reputational risk of the whole group.

29. While variations in the nature of activities, and patterns of relationships between institutions and customers in each sector justify variations in the KYC requirements imposed on each sector, the group should be alert when cross-selling products and services to customers from different business arms that the KYC requirements of the relevant sectors should be applied.

GLOSSARY

Agent One who executes orders for or otherwise acts on behalf of another (the principal), and is subject to its control and authority. The agent takes no financial risk and may receive a fee or commission.

Allocation (give-up) The process of moving the trade from the executing broker to the clearing broker in exchange traded derivatives.

Announcement In a new bond issue, the day on which a release is sent to prospective syndicate members describing the offering and inviting underwriters and selling group members to join the syndicate.

Assets Everything of value that is owned or is due: fixed assets (cash, buildings and machinery) and intangible assets (patents and good will).

Banner option Option with trigger points that activate or de-activate the option.

Bid (a) The price or yield at which a purchaser is willing to buy a given security. (b) To quote a price or yield at which a purchaser is able to buy a given security. (c) The investor's selling price of units in a unit linked policy.

BIS Bank for International Settlements.

Bond A certificate of debt, generally long-term, under the terms of which an issuer contracts, *inter alia*, to pay the holder a fixed principal amount on a stated future date and, usually, a series of interest payments during its life.

Broker An agent, often a member of a stock exchange firm or an exchange member himself who acts as intermediary between buyer and seller. A commission is charged for this service.

Broker/Dealer Firm that operates in dual capacity in the securities market place: as principal trading for its own account and as broker representing clients on the market.

Buying in The action taken by a broker failing to receive delivery of securities from a counterparty on settlement date to purchase these securities in the open market.

Call option An option that gives the seller the right, but not the obligation, to buy a specified quantity of the underlying asset at a fixed price, on or before a specified date. The buyer of a call option has the obligation (because they have bought the right) to make delivery of the underlying asset if the option is exercised by the seller.

Cap Option with a limit embedded in it, above which the holder is reimbursed.

Capital markets A term used to describe the means by which large amounts of money (capital) are raised by companies, governments and other organisations for long-term use and the subsequent trading of the instruments issued in recognition of such capital.

Central securities depository (CSD) An organisation which holds securities in either immobilised or dematerialised form thereby enabling transactions to be processed by book entry transfer. Also provides securities administration services.

Certificate Paper form of shares (or bonds), representing ownership of a company (or its debt).

CHAPS Clearing House Automated Payment System. The clearing system for Sterling and Euro payments between banks.

CHIPS Clearing House Interbank Payments System. The clearing system for US dollar payments between banks in New York.

Clean price The total price of a bond less accrued interest.

Clearing The centralised process whereby transacted business is recorded and positions are maintained.

Clearing house Company that acts as central counterparty for the settlement of stock exchange and derivatives exchange transactions.

Clearing organisation The clearing organisation acts as the guarantor of the performance and settlement of contracts that are traded on an exchange.

Clearnet The clearing house for Euronext.

Clearstream   CSD and clearing house based in Luxembourg and Frankfurt and linked into Deutsche Börse.

Collar   Also Cylinder, Tunnel, Fence or Corridor. The sale of a put (or call) option and purchase of a call (or put) at different strikes (typically both out-of-the-money) or the purchase of a cap combined with the sale of a floor. *See* **Range Forward**.

Collateral   An acceptable asset used to cover a margin requirement.

Commercial paper   Short-term obligations with maturities between 2 and 270 days issued by banks, corporations or other borrowers to investors with temporarily idle cash. They are usually discounted although some are interest-bearing.

Commission   Charge levied by a firm for agency broking.

Comparison   *See* **Matching**.

Confirm   An agreement for each individual OTC transaction which has specific terms.

Contract   The standard unit of trading for futures and options. It is also commonly referred to as a 'lot'.

Convergence   The movement of the cash asset price toward the futures price as the expiration date of the futures contract approaches.

Convertible bond   Security (usually a bond or preferred stock) that can be exchanged for other securities, usually common stock of the same issuer, at the option of the holder and under certain conditions.

Corporate action   One of many possible capital restructuring changes or similar actions taken by the company, which may have an impact on the market price of its securities, and which may require the shareholders to make certain decisions.

Counterparty   A trade can take place between two or more counterparties. Usually one party to a trade refers to its trading partners as counterparties.

Coupon   Generally, the nominal annual rate of interest expressed as a percentage of the principal value. The interest is paid to the holder of a fixed income security by the borrower. The coupon is generally paid annually, semi-annually or in some cases quarterly depending on the type of security.

Credit derivatives   Credit derivatives have as the underlying asset some kind of credit default. As with all derivatives, the credit derivative is designed to enable the risk related to a credit issue, such as non-payment of an interest coupon on a corporate or sovereign bond, or the non-repayment of a loan, to be transferred.

Credit risk   The risk that a borrower, or a counterparty to a deal, or the issuer of a security, will default on repayment or not deliver its side of the deal.

CREST   The organisation in the UK that holds UK and Irish company share in dematerialised form and clears and settles trades in UK and Irish company shares.

Cross-border trading   Trading which takes place between persons or entities from different countries.

CSD   *See* **Central securities depository**.

Currency futures   Contracts calling for delivery of a specific amount of a foreign currency at a specified future date in return for a given amount of say US Dollars.

Currency swap   An agreement to exchange interest related payments in the same currency from fixed rate into floating rate (or vice versa) or from one type of floating rate to another. A currency swap is different to an interest rate swap as the principal amounts are also swapped.

Custodian   Institution holding securities in safekeeping for a client. A custodian also offers different services to its clients (settlement, portfolio services, etc.).

Dealer   Individual or firm that acts as principal in all transactions, buying for his own account.

Default   Failure to perform on a futures contract, either cash settlement or physical settlement.

Delivery versus payment (DVP)   Settlement where transfer of the security and payment for it occur simultaneously.

Derivative   A financial instrument whose value is dependent upon the value of an underlying asset.

Dividend   Distribution of profits made by a company or unit trust to its shareholders if it chooses to do so.

Duration   A measure of the relative volatility of a bond; it is an approximation for the price change of a bond for a given change in the interest rate. Duration is measured in units of time. It includes the effects of time until maturity, cash flows and the yield to maturity.

DVP   *See* **Delivery versus payment**.

Earnings per share Profit of a company divided by the shares in issue.

Emerging market Non-industrialised country with: low or middle per capita income, as published annually by the World Bank; an undeveloped capital market (i.e., the market represents only a small portion of their GDP).

EMS *See* **European Monetary System**.

Endowment policy Form of saving linked with life assurance. Must be held for at least 10 years to get full benefit.

EPS *See* **Earnings per share**.

Equity A common term to describe stocks or shares.

Euro The name of the single European currency.

Eurobond An interest-bearing security issued across national borders, usually issued in a currency other than that of the issuer's home country. Because there is no regulatory protection, only governments and top rated multinational corporations can issue Eurobonds that the market will accept.

Euroclear A book-entry clearing facility for most Eurocurrency and foreign securities. Linked to Euronext through the acquisition of SICOVAM and the recently announced merger with CREST.

Euronext A pan-European securities and derivatives exchange listing Dutch, French, Portuguese and Belgium securities and derivatives plus the derivative products traded on LIFFE.

Euronext.liffe *See* **London International Financial Futures and Options Exchange**.

Exchange Market place for trading.

Exchange rate The rate at which one currency can be exchanged for another.

Execution The action of trading in the markets.

Financial Services Authority UK financial services regulator.

Fixed income Interest on a security which is calculated as a constant specified percentage of the principal amount and paid at the end of specified interest periods, usually annually or semi-annually, until maturity.

Floor A package of interest rate options whereby, at each of a series of future fixing dates, if an agreed reference rate such as LIBOR is lower than the strike rate, the option buyer receives the difference between them, calculated on an agreed notional principal amount for the period until the next fixing date. *See* **Cap, Collar**.

Foreign exchange (forex or FX)   Exchange of one currency into another.

Forex   *See* **Foreign exchange**.

Forward Rate Agreement (FRA)   An agreement where the client can fix the rate of interest that will be applied to a notional loan or deposit, drawn or placed on an agreed date in the future, for a specified term.

Forwards   These are very similar to futures contracts but they are not mainly traded on an exchange. They are not marked to market daily but settled only on the delivery date.

FRA   *See* **Forward Rate Agreement**.

FSA   *See* **Financial Services Authority**.

Fund manager   Individuals or specialist companies responsible for investing the assets of a fund in such a way as to maximise its value. They do this by following a strategy to buy and sell equities and other financial instruments.

Future   An agreement to buy or sell an asset at a certain time in the future for a certain price.

Future value   The value of something at a point in the future.

Global custodian   Institution that safekeeps, settles and performs processing of income collection, tax reclaim, multicurrency reporting, cash management, foreign exchange, corporate action and proxy monitoring, etc., for clients' securities in all required market places.

Group   If one company controls one or more other companies, they are collectively a group.

Group of 30 (G30)   Private international organisation aiming to deepen understanding of international economic and financial issues. Established in 1978, it is a private, non-profit international body composed of very senior representatives of the private and public sectors and academia.

Hedging   A trading method which is designed to reduce or mitigate risk (e.g., reducing the risk of a cash position using a derivative instrument to offset the price movement of the cash asset). A broader definition of hedging includes using derivatives as a temporary substitute for the cash or asset position.

Holding company A company which owns more than 50% of the shares of another company as its holding company. *See also* **Subsidiary**.

Integration The third stage of money laundering, in which the money is finally integrated into the legitimate economy. *See also* **Placement**, **Layering**.

Interest rate futures Based on a debt instrument such as a government bond or a Treasury Bill as the underlying product it requires the delivery of a bond or bill to fulfil the contract.

Interest rate swap An agreement to exchange interest related payments in the same currency from fixed rate into floating rate (or vice versa) or from one type of floating rate to another.

Intervention The process whereby the Bank of England acts to influence the exchange rate for sterling by buying it to support its value or selling it to weaken it.

Investments Items defined in the FSA 1986 to be regulated by it. Includes shares, Bonds, options, Futures, life assurance and pensions.

ISDA International Swaps and Derivatives Association, previously known as the International Swap Dealers Association. Many market participants use ISDA documentation.

ISSA The International Securities Services Association.

Issue Stocks or Bonds sold by a corporation or government entity at a particular time.

Issuer Legal entity that issues and distributes securities.

ISMA International Securities Markets Association.

Layering Stage in the process of money laundering.

LCH London Clearing House.

Liquidity A liquid asset is one that can be converted easily and rapidly into cash without a substantial loss of value.

Liquidity risk The risk that a bank may not be able to close out a position because the market is illiquid.

Listed company Company which has been admitted to listing on a stock exchange and whose shares can then be dealt on that exchange.

Listed securities Securities listed on a stock exchange are tradeable on this exchange.

Local An individual member of an exchange who trades solely for their own account.

Local currency   Currency of the country of settlement.

London International Financial Futures and Options Exchange (LIFFE)   Market for trading in Bonds, interest rates, FTSE 100 Index and FTSE Mid 250 Index, Futures, plus equity options and soft commodity derivatives, now part of Euronext.

Long   A bought position in a derivative which is held open.

Long position   Refers to an investor's account in which he has more shares of a specific security than he needs to meet his settlement obligations.

M&A   *See* **Mergers and acquisitions.**

Margin   Initial margin is collateral placed by one party with a counterparty or clearing house at the time of a deal, against the possibility that the market price will move against the first party, thereby leaving the counterparty with a credit risk. Variation margin is a payment made, or collateral transferred, from one party to the other because the market price of the transaction or of collateral has changed. Variation margin payment is either in effect a settlement of profit/loss (e.g., in the case of a futures contract) or the reduction of credit exposure. In a loan, margin is the extra interest above a benchmark such as LIBOR required by a lender to compensate for the credit risk of that particular borrower. Money or assets that must be deposited by participants in securities lending, repos or OTC derivatives markets as a guarantee that they will be able to meet their commitments at the due date.

Market   Description of any organisation or facility through which items are traded. All exchanges are markets.

Market maker   A trader who works for an organisation such as an investment bank. They quote bids and offers in the market and are normally under an obligation to make a price in a certain number of contracts. They create Liquidity in the contract by offering to buy or sell.

Market price   In the case of a security, the market price is usually considered as the last reported price at which the stock or bond has been sold.

Market risk   The risk that the market value of a position falls. Also known as *Position Risk*.

Market value   The price at which a security is trading and could presumably be purchased or sold.

Master agreement   This agreement is for OTC transactions and is signed between the client and the broker. It covers the basic terms under which the client and broker wish to transact business. Each individual trade has a separate individual agreement with specific terms known as a Confirm.

Matching   A system to compare trades and ensure that both sides of trade correspond. Also known as *Checking* or *Comparison.*

Maturity   The date on which the Principal Value or Nominal Value of a Bond becomes due and payable in full to the holder.

Mergers and acquisitions (M&A)   Division of securities houses or merchant banks responsible for advising on take-over activity. Usually works with the corporate finance department and is often kept as a single unit.

Money laundering   The process where criminals attempt to conceal the true origin and ownership of the proceeds of their criminal activities and to legitimise these proceeds by introducing them into the mainstream of financial activities.

Money market   The market for the purchase and sale of short-term financial instruments. Short term is usually defined as less than one year.

Mortgage   A form of security on borrowing commonly associated with home borrowing.

Mutual fund   Fund operated by an investment company that raises money from shareholders and invests it in stocks, bonds or other instruments (e.g., unit trust, investment fund, SICAV).

Naked option   An option bought or sold for speculation, with no offsetting existing position behind it.

Net Present Value (NPV)   The net total of several present values (arising from cashflows at different future dates) added together, some of which may be positive and some negative.

Netting   Trading partners offset their positions, thereby reducing the number of positions for settlement. Netting can be either *Bilateral, Multilateral* or *Continuous Net Settlement.*

Nostro   A bank's nostro account is its currency account held with a foreign bank.

Note   Bonds issued with a relatively short maturity are often called notes.

Offer price   The price at which a trader or market maker is willing to sell a contract.

Online Processing which is executed via an interactive input onto a PC or stationary terminal connected to a processing centre.

Open outcry The style of trading whereby traders face each other in a designated area such as a pit and shout or call their respective bids and offers. Hand signals are also used to communicate. It is governed by exchange rules.

Operational risk The risk of losses resulting from inadequate systems and control, human errors or management failings.

Option An option is, in the case of the buyer, the right, but not the obligation, to take (call) or make (put) for delivery of the underlying product; in the case of the seller it is the obligation to make or take delivery of the underlying product.

OTC *See* **Over-the-counter.**

Over-the-counter (OTC) A one-to-one agreement between two counterparties where the specifications of the product are completely flexible and non-standardised.

Overdraft Withdrawal of more money than is in a bank account at a given time.

Placement Stage in the process of money laundering.

Pit The designated area on the market floor where a particular contract is traded. It may be termed a ring in some markets (e.g., LME).

Portfolio List of investments held by an individual or company, or list of loans made by a bank or financial institution.

Position risk *See* **Market risk.**

Present value The amount of money which needs to be invested (or borrowed) now at a given interest rate in order to achieve exactly a given cashflow in the future, assuming compound reinvestment (or re-funding) of any interest payments received (or paid) before the end. *See* **Future value.**

Pre-settlement Checks and procedures undertaken immediately after execution of a trade prior to Settlement.

Principal trading When a member firm of the *London Stock Exchange* buys stock from or sells stock to a non-member.

Real time gross settlement (RTGS) Gross settlement system where trades are settled continuously through the processing day.

Reconciliation The comparison of a person's records of cash and securities position with records held by another party and the investigation and resolution of any discrepancies between the two sets of records.

Reorganisation Generally any event where the equity, debt or capital structure of a company is changed.

Repo *See* **Repurchase agreement.**

Repurchase agreement (repo) Borrowing funds by providing a government security for collateral and promising to 'repurchase' the security at the end of the agreed upon time period. The associated interest rate is the 'repo-rate'.

Reputational risk The risk that an organisation's reputation will be damaged.

Safekeeping Holding of securities on behalf of clients. They are free to sell at any time.

Securities Bonds and equities.

Securities lending Loan of securities by an investor to another (usually a broker–dealer), usually to cover a short sale.

Settlement date The date on which a trade is cleared by delivery of securities against funds (actual settlement date, contractual settlement date).

Short A sold position in a derivative which is held open.

Short sale The sale of securities not owned by the seller in the expectation that the price of these securities will fall or as part of an arbitrage.

Short selling Selling stock that you do not own.

SGX The merged central Stock Exchange of Singapore & SIMEX.

Speculation A deal undertaken because the dealer expects prices to move in his favour and thereby realise a profit.

Speculator The speculator is a trader who wants to assume risk for potentially much higher rewards.

Stock In some countries (e.g., US), the term applies to ordinary share capital of a company. In other countries (e.g., UK), stock may mean share capital that is issued in variable amounts instead of in fixed specified amounts, or it can describe government loans.

Subsidiary A separate part of a business.

Swap Arrangement where two borrowers, one of whom has fixed interest and one of whom has floating rate borrowings, swap their commitments with each other. A bank would arrange the swap and charge a fee.

SWIFT Society for Worldwide Interbank Financial Telecommunications. Secure electronic communications network between banks.

Takeover When one company obtains more than 50% of another company's shares.

Time value The amount by which an option's premium exceeds its intrinsic value. If an option has no intrinsic value, the premium consists entirely of time value.

Trade date The date on which a trade is made.

Trader An individual who buys and sells securities with the objective of making short-term gains.

Transfer Change of ownership of securities.

TRAX Trade confirmation system for the Euromarkets operated by ISMA. *See* **ISMA.**

Treasury Arm of Government responsible for all financial decisions and regulation of the financial services sector.

Treasury bill Money market instrument with a life of less than one year issued by the US and UK governments.

Trigger option *See* **Barrier option.**

Trust A legal arrangement where one person (the trustee) holds property (the trust property) on behalf of one or more other persons (the beneficiaries).

Unit trust A system whereby money from a number of investors is pooled together and invested collectively on their behalf. Each owns a unit (or number of them), the value of which depends on the value of those items owned by the trust.

Value at Risk (VaR) The maximum amount which a bank expects to lose, with a given confidence level, over a given time period.

VaR *See* **Value at Risk.**

Volatility The degree of scatter of the underlying price when compared with the mean average rate.

Vostro A vostro account is another bank's account held at our bank in our currency.

With-profits policy An endowment or whole life policy which participates in the investment performance of the life company through the allocation of normal and terminal bonuses.

Yield Internal rate of return expressed as a percentage.

ABBREVIATIONS

. . . .

AIMA	Alternative Investment Management Association
AML	Anti Money Laundering
AUTIF	Association of Unit Trust Investment Funds
BCBS	Basel Committee on Banking Supervision
BIS	Bank for International Settlement
CDD	Customer Due Diligence
CDD	*General Guide to Account Opening and Customer Identification*
CCP	Central Clearing counterParty
CHAPS	Clearing House Automated Payment System
CHIPS	Clearing House Interbank Payment System
CLS	Continuous Linked Settlement
COB	Conduct Of Business
CREST	UK Central Securities Depository
CSD	Central Securities Depository
DVD	Delivery Versus Delivery
DVP	Delivery Versus Payment
ESAAMLG	Eastern and Southern Africa Anti-Money Laundering Group
FATF	Financial Action Task Force
FIU	Financial Intelligence Unit
FSA	Financial Services Authority
FX	Foreign eXchange
GAFI	Groupe d'Action FInancière
G30	Group of Thirty
GSCS	Benchmarking company
HR	Human Resource
ISDA	International Swaps and Derivatives Association

ISMA	International Securities Markets Association
ISSA	International Securities Services Association
IT	Information Technology
KYC	Know Your Client
LCH	London Clearing House
LIFFE	London International Financial Futures Exchange
LSE	London Stock Exchange
LTCM	Long Term Capital Management
LVFTS	Large-value Funds Transfer System
M&A	Mergers and Acquisitions
MI	Management Information
MIS	Management Information System
ML	Money Laundering
NCCT	Non-Cooperative Countries and Territories
OM	The Swedish Exchange
OTC	Over The Counter
P&L	Profit and Loss
Repo	Repurchase agreement
RFP	Request For Proposal
RMG	Risk Management Group
SIA	Securities Industry Association
STP	Straight-Through-Processing
SWIFT	Society for Worldwide Interbank Financial Telecommunications
T&D	Training and Development
TRAX	Bond matching system
UCITS	Undertakings for Collective Investment in Transferable Securities
VaR	Value at Risk

USEFUL WEBSITES AND SUGGESTED FURTHER READING

....

WEBSITES

www.bba.org.uk (British Bankers Association)
www.bis.org (Bank for International Settlement)
www.clearstream.com
www.cls-group.com (CLS Bank)
www.euroclear.com
www.euronext.com
www.fatf-gafi.org (Financial Action Task Force)
www.foa.co.uk (Futures and Options Association)
www.fsa.gov.uk (Financial Services Authority)
www.fundadmin.com (Bank of New York)
www.iccwbo.org (International Chamber of Commerce)
www.isda.org (International Swaps and Derivatives Association)
www.isla.co.uk (International Securities Lending Association)
www.isma.co.uk (International Securities Markets Association)
www.issanet.org (International Securities Services Association)
www.liffe.com
www.londonstockexchange.com
www.sii.org.uk (The Securities and Investment Institute)

SUGGESTED FURTHER READING

- *Understanding the Financial Markets**
- *Managing Technology in the Operations Function**
- *Clearing, Settlement and Custody**
- *Controls Procedures and Risk**
- *Relationship and Resource Management in Operations**
- *Clearing and Settlement of Derivatives*

Published by Butterworth Heinemann

- *Mastering Treasury Operations*
- *Understanding Foreign Exchange and Currency Options*

Published by FT Prentice Hall

- *Fundamentals of Global Operations Management*, Second Edition, by David Loader
- *An Introduction to Credit Derivatives*, by David Loader
- *Securities Operations: A Guide to Trade and Position Management*, by Michael Simmons

Published by John Wiley & Sons

visUlearn™ SERIES OF CD-ROMs

- *Equities & Bonds*
- *Derivatives & Commodities*
- *Operations – Clearing, Settlement & Custody*
- *An Overview of the Financial Services Industry*

*Order from *www.dscporfolio.com* or call 0207 403 8383 quoting 'websites/reading' for a major discount.

INDEX